CHRIST PREËMINENT

Seeing the King's Face and Living Like the Master to be Ready for His Return

by
H.E. SCHMUL

Author of
Forgiving Love: The Power to Change the Past and The Power to Control the Future

"And he is the head of the body, the church; who is the beginning, the firstborn from the dead; that in all things he might have the preëminence."
—Colossians 1:18—

"I would be a Christian if it were not for the Christians."
—Mahatma Gandhi—

SCHMUL PUBLISHING COMPANY
NICHOLASVILLE, KENTUCKY

COPYRIGHT © 2002 BY SCHMUL PUBLISHING CO.
All rights reserved. No part of this publication may be reproduced or used in any form or by any means—graphic, electronic, or mechanical, including photocopying, recording, taping, or information storage or retrieval systems—without prior written permission of the publishers.

Churches and other noncommercial interests may reproduce portions of this book without prior written permission of the publisher, provided such quotations are not offered for sale—or other compensation in any form—whether alone or as part of another publication, and provided that the text does not exceed 500 words or five percent of the entire book, whichever is less, and does not include material quoted from another publisher. When reproducing text from this book, the following credit line must be included: "From *Christ Preëminent: Seeing the King's Face and Living Like the Master to be Ready for His Return* by H.E. Schmul, © 2002 by Schmul Publishing Co., Nicholasville, Kentucky. Used by permission."

Published by Schmul Publishing Co.
PO Box 776
Nicholasville, KY USA

Printed in the United States of America

ISBN 10: 0-88019-446-4
ISBN 13: 978-0-88019-446-4

Visit us on the Internet at www.wesleyanbooks.com, or order direct from the publisher by calling 800-772-6657, or by writing to the above address.

Contents

Preface 4

PART I: CHRIST PREËMINENT 5
   1 *The Head of the Church* 5
   2 *Muddy and Oily Waters* 10
   3 *The Heart of the Church* 15
   4 *The Hope of the Church* 22

PART II: LET ME SEE THE KING'S FACE 28
   5 *The Difference Between Christians* 28
   6 *Moses the Incomparable* 32
   7 *Paul the Inexhaustible* 37
   8 *Mary the Indomitable* 42

PART III: LIVING LIKE THE MASTER 47
   9 *The Greatest Trials Come From our Brethren* 47
   10 *Earthen Vessels?* 52
   11 *What Follows the Spear?* 57
   12 *Joseph and His Brethren* 60

PART IV: THE TEN VIRGINS 67
   13 *More Alike than Unlike* 67
   14 *A Shared Expectancy* 72
   15 *The Time of Night* 78
   16 *The Tragedy of the Time* 84

Preface

"THAT IN ALL THINGS He might have the preëminence," was one of the controlling principles of H. E. Schmul's life. These words were inscribed on a banner in the church he pastored; more importantly, they were written in the chambers of his mind and embedded in the depth of his soul. Out of that passion for Christ and his sincere desire to exalt him as the head of the Church comes this powerful book. It is H.E. Schmul at his best—vintage preaching material from one of the twentieth century's premier holiness evangelists. If you are looking for clear, anointed, hard-hitting truth, *this is it!*

H.E. Schmul states about the Church of our day: "We have missed it tremendously when we have failed through the years to preach the preëminence of Christ in His Church. He is the heart of the Church— He is not only the head of it, but He is the heart of it." In this inspiring treatise, Brother Schmul uncovers the implications of what it means for Christ to be preëminent. It brings into focus the proper relationships between human leadership and divine authority in the Church. The author of the book challenges us to keep the King's face in view and to maintain spiritual readiness for His appearing.

Reading this material reminded me of the indebtedness we have to H.E. Schmul, co-founder with H. Robb French of the Interchurch Holiness Convention, successful pastor, eminent evangelist, mentor, and friend. Schmul Publishing Company is to be commended for their decision to make these messages available to the reading public. I recommend the book to earnest Christians who seek to make Christ preëminent in their lives, homes, and church.

—LEONARD SANKEY
*General Secretary,
InterChurch Holiness Convention
2002*

PART I
CHRIST PREËMINENT

1
The Head of the Church

THE BOOK OF COLOSSIANS is a very wonderful and beautiful book. In this book we see that Christ is preëminent. Christ is preëminent in creation. Christ is also preëminent at the cross. And for our consideration now I would like to talk about, "Christ Preëminent in His Church."

Now, I belong to the Wesleyan Methodist Church, but I am so very happy I can report to you that I belong to something bigger than the Wesleyan Methodist Church. I belong to the glorious Church. His Church. Praise God.

The Church Before Time

The Church was in the heart and the mind of God long before a lot of people think it was. The Church was in the heart and mind of God long before the first speck of dust floated in remotest space. Long before the first mountains were piled up in their grandeur and rugged splendor. Long before God ever capped some of them with perpetual snows. Long before He ever carpeted the earth with green and tacked it down with daffodils and daisies. Long before Jesus was cradled in the arms of the Virgin Mary. Long before the Master trod the dusty roads of this old world. Long before He groaned in Gethsemane. Long before He cried, "It is finished," on Calvary. Long before He burst out of the darkness of the tomb into the light of the Easter morning, the Church was in the heart and the mind of God.

The Church had always been near and dear to the heart of the Father. The Church had always been near and dear to the heart of His Son. I feel that it is time we endeavor to give the Church its rightful and proper place in the plan and economy and program of God.

Christ is the head of the Church. Christ is the heart of His church. And Christ is the only hope of the Church.

Now for some reason or other, there are people in the world, especially men and women in the place of leadership, who get rather nervous when you begin to speak about Christ being preëminent in His Church. They articulate in opposition to such themes and idea. They seem to feel that, if you exalt Jesus to His place, His rightful place, His God-given place, the created place the Father had in mind for Him, you are taking something away from them, you are taking something of their power. Bishops, superintendents, moderators, generals and even some pastors and others get rather nervous and upset when you exalt the authority and power and rightful place of Christ as the head of His church.

But, beloved, long before the first pope ever ruled, the first board ever sat, the first bishop ever begun to boss anybody around, or the first superintendents began to move this direction and that direction; long before your general conferences ever sat or your annual assemblies ever met; long before the first block was ever laid on the banks of the Tiber where fallen apostates have ruled through the dusty centuries of the past; long before the gleam of a denominational program ever flashed in any modern man's eye, God ordained that Christ should be the head of His Church, and God is jealous concerning Christ being the head of that Church. Christ has never relegated that authority to another. He has never abdicated that power or given it to anyone else. God is jealous that His Son be enshrined in our hearts as our head individually and as the head of His Church collectively.

His Church is bigger than any two-by-four organization, whether it is located in Rome or Mecca or Winona Lake or Marion or Indianapolis or what have you. It is bigger than all we have put together, and it is high time that church leaders put Jesus Christ back as the head and the heart of His own work and His own program. If their programs ever are to thrive, if their programs ever are to be blessed, and if their programs are ever to get out of the long deep rut they have been digging for endless, countless centuries, it will be only when they turn their faces toward God and Christ, acknowledge Him as the King of kings and the Lord or lords and put Him back as the head of His Church. Hallelujah!

I do not think I am taking anything away from anybody or treating anybody's office or position lightly when I say that Jesus is the head of the Church. I owe my allegiance first and last to Jesus Christ as the head of the Church. And I am more concerned about pleasing Him as the head of the Church than I am about pleasing anybody else.

I feel, personally, that we are taking nothing away from the recognized and elected leaders of the church world today, whether they are holiness leaders or others. I feel we are taking absolutely nothing away from them, but we are giving back to Jesus Christ everything that is rightfully His and which rightfully belongs to Him. No movement shall grow, whether it is the holiness movement or any other movement, until it honors and glorifies and puts Christ back as the head of the Church. Hallelujah! Glory to God.

The Source of Power

Now when we speak of Christ being the head of the Church, we think of the head as the source of authority and power. Notice what he tells us in this chapter. He says, "Who hath delivered us from the power of darkness and hath translated us into the kingdom of His dear Son."

Now here is power. Here is a holy power. There are powers of light, and there are powers of darkness. And Jesus Christ alone as the head of the Church has the power to translate us out of the kingdom of darkness, out of the kingdom of night, out of the kingdom of hell, into the glorious kingdom of light and power and righteousness.

The trouble today is that a lot of our people, young people as well as others, have met with leaders of the church, superintendents, bishops, and district elders. They have been approved by a lot of high sounding titled men of the church, but their lives are unchanged and they are not transformed because they have never met the head of the Church.

My advice to every young person, no matter if he is a fourth generation holiness individual, a fifth generation Methodist or a first generation Free Methodist, is never stop with meeting the bishop, never stop with meeting the superintendent, never stop with meeting the official board, but never stop until you meet Jesus Christ, the head of the Church. When he has a face to face and heart to heart confrontation with the blessed and adorable son of God, he will never get over it and he will never get away from it. Hallelujah! Christ is the head of the church.

Now that may make some of you folks a little bit nervous and you may be a little bit upset about it, but I want to enshrine Jesus Christ once and for all in your mind as the true head of His Church.

A lot of young people in our holiness churches are good young people. They are clean young people. They do not have a lot of bad or vicious habits. But they have never met Jesus Christ as the head of the Church. They can meet the official board and the welcoming committee. The bishop himself can open the door and take them in, make them welcome, pump their hands and tell them how wonderful they are. But they will never be satisfied until they meet Jesus Christ, the head of the Church.

Meeting the Head of the Church

I remember in my own life how powerless I was, how weak I was, how fearful I was in nature and disposition, desiring to live a good life, desiring to live a better life, but one night I knelt at the altar, met the head of the Church Himself, and I have never been the same from then until this good hour.

I had been in trouble with law enforcement. I had been in trouble with society. They used retraining bands and forces, tried to modify my life, reform me and work me over, but instead of getting better I was getting constantly worse. But that night when I bent my humble knees in His presence, I had a person to person confrontation with Jesus Christ, the head of the Church.

It was an epochal relationship in my life. Something happened that night. All of a sudden out of my darkness, out of my weakness, out of my sinfulness, out of the fetters that had tied me, I found myself translated into the kingdom of His dear Son. I found myself in a new land. I found myself in a new world. I had met Someone beside the church board. I had met Someone beside a leader in the church. I had gotten past them all. I had met Jesus Christ. I had met the master for myself.

These men had no power to change me. These men had no power to help. But *He* had power. *He* was the head of the thing. *He* put me in, and no one else can put me out. Hallelujah! Glory be to God.

Oh, they can scratch out my name, they can cross it out and they can scandalize it. They can put me on the outside. They can kick me out as trash, as the offscouring of the earth. They can wash their hands of me, and they can dismiss me completely. But that is a far cry from being put out by the head of the Church.

"As many as received Him to them gave He authority, to them gave He the power to become the sons of God, to as many as believed on His name."

I felt a new dynamic come into my life. I felt a new power take hold of me. The things I once loved I now hated. The things I once adored, I now revolted against. I found a new source of affection and love, and the things I once despised I now embraced. The crowd I once hated I followed everywhere across the country, seeking their fellowship, reveling in their counsel, delighting in their prayers. And anxious for their "well done."

2
Muddy and Oily Waters

THE CHRIST IS THE head of the church. Not only does headship symbolize authority, but it also symbolizes revelation. Christ the head of the church. From Him we receive all true revelation.

You know, we are living in rather a muddy day, a complicated day. The religious waters are muddy waters today. The religious streams of thought are polluted. The waters are oily and brown and mixed and muddied and unsanitary. The theologians and the doctors and the denominational leaders have been muddying the waters. Millions and billions of words have been preached and positions innumerable and multiplied have been taken again and again. "This is right and that is wrong. That is wrong and this is right."

A number of years ago a church would vote this or that position—this is where we stand on the wedding ring, on all jewelry, on the movies, or on something else. Twenty years ago they stood there on that question. And twenty years ago they stood over here on this question. But men that told us where to stand then are now telling us the very contrary now. Folk are in confusion. The waters are muddy and oily, and folk come to preachers asking, "What is right? What is wrong? What shall I do? Who can I believe?"

Millions of words are printed. Billions of words are spoken, and the air is filled with confusion. Folk do not know what to believe. They do not know from whom to seek counsel.

Sad to say, through the centuries, there has been a tendency on the part of people to lean on the church to make every interpretation. That is the trouble today. This papal infallibility that started on the banks of the apostate Tiber has now found its way into the degrees and orders and the meeting of groups that are now making up our minds for us and becoming our conscience for us. The tragedy is that they are contradicting themselves, saying that things which they told us were wrong twenty years ago are right, now.

I like what a certain brother has to say on that point. He says, "When did they lie? Were they lying to me twenty years ago when I had to give up the movies and the world and the flesh and the devil, or are they lying to me today when they tell me that the world and the flesh and the devil and compromise and the rest of it is right? *When did they lie?*"

There is a Source of Authority

Notice the lesson here. Paul is praying. He is praying for the Colossian church as individuals. "I do not cease to pray for you. I desire that ye be filled with a knowledge of His will. That you have all wisdom and all spiritual understanding and that you would walk worthy of the Lord and please Him and that you would increase in the knowledge of God."

My friend, there are some people that are not in the dark. Some folk are not in a cloud. Some people have not been caught in the vortex of this confusion and carried down the old intellectual-theological stream of confusion and doubt and despair. Some people have kept their minds and hearts clear.

How do you account for it? Here is how you account for it: Jesus Christ is the head of the Church. And the Apostle Paul here is praying for these Colossians. "I am praying for you that each of you will press your way through until you are filled with the knowledge of His will in real spiritual understanding and in personal experience and that you keep increasing in the knowledge of God."

If you want to get a drink out of the religious stream today, I tell you it is hard to find a place where the stream is not oily and confused and where the waters are not muddy. Consequently, there is a thirsty world out there that would like to slake its thirst, but they cannot find a place to get a clear, pure drink. They cannot get some things settled in their minds. They still ask, "Is it right or is it wrong?"

I like to travel in the field. I like to go hunting. I like to get out in the field especially in the fall time, and if I am hunting and it is hot and I am dry and weary and tired, I tell you, friends, I do not stop for a drink down on the low side of the farmer's pig pen or where the cattle have been running up and down through the stream and the hogs have been making a mire in the middle of the pond. No, sir! Not on the flats and the lowlands and the swamps do I stop and invite infection by drinking where wiggletails are spawned and polliwogs are born and snakes make their nests and where the rest of the lizards and the crawling things live. No, sir.

The Fountainhead

I skirt around the pigpen and I get on the other side of the cattle barn and I start heading for that old mountain back up there that is crested with snow. I know that this muddy place down here is not the source. I think I will find the source somewhere. I will keep traveling. I will walk up the hillside. I will crawl under the last line fence. Get past the district superintendent. Get past the general superintendent and climb past the last bishop and get up there where the heavenly light begins to flow. Where the waters are melted. Where the perpetual snows are. I will keep traveling until I get there. Where the water begins to bubble free and fresh out of the hillsides of divine revelation. With my spiritual gun over my arm I will find a cool place by the stream. I will get on my knees. I will tarry there. I will wait until a fresh revelation breaks in on my soul, until some things are settled in my heart for time and for eternity. Blessed be God. I will get something from the fountainhead of revelation, the fountainhead of all knowledge, the fountainhead of divine inspiration. I will get the last word from Him. I will hear the final Amen. I will get the crossing of every "t" and the dotting of every "i" and every jot and every tittle from the heart and from the head of the Church Himself. I will settle this thing, by the grace of God.

When you come down from there you have some things settled that can never be shaken. You have increased in knowledge and understanding. You can look the general or the bishop in the face and kindly tell them, "As for me and my house, sirs, we will serve the Lord. This is the way we are taking." Hallelujah.

I am talking about Christ being the head of His Church. Oh, I am so glad that is the way it is. Praise God! No papal infallibility for me.

Here is the divine revelation. I will live where the water is clear. I will not get my drinks down here in the polliwog pond. And that is what you need to do, friend. There are some things you can settle for yourself. You do not need to wait for anybody else to settle them for you. You can crawl up that mountain yourself. You can get some things settled for time and for eternity. Once you are really transformed you can settle some things for yourself. You can set your face like a flint and not deviate to the left hand nor to the right hand. And when the waters get muddy again, blessed be God, you will know where to find a solution to your problem. You will know where the answer to every question is to be found—it is in Christ, the head of the Church.

Coming Under the Right Authority

This is what many men in leadership today call insubordination. This is insubordination of the purest kind—to make Christ supreme authority. Oh, they do not say so publicly, but their attitude is, "to flaunt our rules and to disregard our decisions and our bounds and our recommendations and not be loyal to our church and our program means that you cannot be a good pastor or district leader or whatever. You will have to give us more loyalty. You will have to pay your budgets. You will have to come under."

Well, my friend, I do not have to come under. I have thought this matter over with the head of the Church, and He tells me that He is the final authority. He informs me that He is the final word. He tells me that He is the alpha and that He is the omega. That He is the beginning of wisdom and that He is the end of divine understanding. Christ is the head of His Church. Do you believe that? Glory be to God. Hallelujah! You can settle some of these things for yourself.

I well remember when this period came in my own life. I was born and raised in the confines of the Allegheny Conference. I thank God for my spiritual birth among these brethren. But I got outside of the conference. I got out on my own where the things I was taught were called into question and where these things were called into disrepute and contention. What would I do? I had heard the stock answers. In my heart I believed them. I felt these things were right, but I did not really know some things for myself. What did I do? I thank God I saw them in the light of divine revelation. I saw this glorious truth that I, for myself, could settle some things. And so I have some things settled today that the Allegheny Conference does not need to settle and the Wesleyan Methodist Church does not need to legislate about. Hallelujah! Blessed be God.

Here is a fence that is higher than any that I have need to build. It is enclosed with divine love. You do not have to have a special, fine, mesh wire to keep folks that have this kind of revelation on the inside. Hallelujah. And you do not have to have a lot of special "do's" and "don't's" to keep the "don't" from getting in from the outside. I am talking about one that is the head of the Church. He has power to take you in, and He alone has power to put you out.

3
The Heart of the Church

CHRIST IS THE HEART of His Church. He tells us in verse seventeen, "He is before all things and by Him all things consist."

The verse preceding that speaks of His creation. "By Him are all things created that are in heaven and that are in earth." Visible thrones, principalities, powers—all things were created by Him. And all things were created for Him, and He is before all things, and by Him all things are held together. All things consist.

That puts Christ at the heart of His universe. That puts Christ at the heart of the system of divine redemption. That puts Christ at the heart of His Church.

If you could go out here with a pick and shovel and tear the mountains down rock by rock and leaf by leaf and stone by stone, at the heart of it all you would find Christ. If you could turn the oceans upside down and dip them out of their beds, at the heart of them all you would find Christ. If you could take yourself through the universe, star by star and galaxy by galaxy, when you hit the heart of it, there you would find Christ.

He is the heart of it all. We have missed it tremendously when we have failed through the years to preach the preëminence of Christ in His church. He is the heart of the Church. *He* is the heart of it. He is not only the head of it, but He is the heart of it.

The Center

When you speak about the heart of a thing, you speak of the center of a thing, the source of its life, the source of its love. The heart of the Church is Christ.

The heart of heaven is Christ. The center of all interests and the center of all activity through all the ages is Christ. When John saw the open door in heaven, what did he see? He said, "I see a Lamb slain in the midst of the throne."

He is in the middle of everything. There in heaven, in the middle of everything in His creation, in the middle of everything in His Church. He may not be the center of your church. He may not be the center of your morning worship. He may not be the center of your prayer meeting. But when it comes to His Church, my friend—not your church, not my church, but *His* Church—Christ is the center.

There He is in the heavens. The angels and the cherubim are all pointing in one direction. They form a tremendous circle around the throne. In the center of that circle is Christ. All the thoughts of the Father through the centuries, every groan the Father ever emits, every sob or sorrow the Father ever has, every thought that God the Father has concerning our salvation, is centered in Christ. Everything is Christ. Everything is Christ and it belongs to Christ. He created all and by Him were all things created. He is the heart of it. He is the center of it. He is the cement that holds this thing together. Glory be to God! Take Him out, and what do you have?

Has Christ Been Taken out of the Church?

Sad to say, today He is not the heart of a good many local and denominational churches. He is not the heart. A good many preachers on Sunday morning say, "Well, come out to our church and meet Christ."

No. You do not go to church to meet Christ. You will not find a church where you find Christ. Just because you have a lofty steeple and a fine tower and a beautiful carpeted aisle and cushioned pews and a pealing organ and a running piano and a fancy choir director and a scholarly D.D. behind the pulpit is no sign you will find Christ in the church. He is probably on the outside knocking on the door.

"If any man will come out of here He will hear My voice and I will come in to his heart. I will sup with him."

Christ is the heart of the Church. That means He is the center of it. He is the creator of its life. He is the cause of its life. He is the sustainer of its life. He is the perpetuator of its life. Wherever you find Christ you find life. This is life—life abundant.

Now if your church is dead it is because there is no Christ. If your services are dead it is because there is no Christ. If your prayer meetings are dead, it is because there is no Christ. If your camp meeting is dead, it is because there is no Christ. Wherever you find a thumping, throbbing, pulsating heart you find life and you find growth and you find development.

Our bodies reproduce themselves every seven years. Why? Because of the faithful organ, the heart, that pushes the blood out to the fingertips, that creates the bones and muscle and gristle and hair.

Christ is the heart of the church, and I am sure to tell you, my dear friends, that the church that has Christ as its heart is a live church. It is a living church. It is a growing church. It is a producing church. It is alive to God. Hallelujah.

Can you imagine death reigning where the Prince of Life lives? Can you imagine things being dead where the Prince of Glory reigns in power? Can you imagine the atmosphere of a funeral parlor and the smell of fancy roses and the presence of innumerable corpses where the presence of Jesus Christ is? I should say not! He is the resurrection and the life.

He is the life

He spoke the word and the seas were filled with swarming fishes. He spoke the word and the hillsides and countrysides were filled with beasts of the field. He spoke the word and Adam became a living soul. Glory be to God. He breathed forth the Holy Ghost on the day of Pentecost. The spirit of Christ is in the world in the presence of the Holy Ghost. And He is here to make us alive. Where Christ is the head and center of a church, that church is alive. Their prayers are alive. Their testimonies are alive. Their giving is alive. Their living is alive. They are alive unto God.

But sad to say most churches' fire and life are not on the heart line. The average church program is not built on this heart line, with Christ as the heart of the church. You can go to a lot of churches on Sunday morning and be easily fooled. You will find a large Sunday school—200 or 300 or 400 or maybe 1000 out to Sunday school. Oh, you might find that the preacher is rather a popular fellow, has a rather interesting manner, sort of flair for a little show, you know, and rather an attractive sort of fellow—a good backslapper, a good mixer, and one who preaches a very fine fundamental Gospel, but is very sure to pull all the teeth out of the truth.

The preacher is sane and sensible. That means he has a straight gun, but he does not have any powder. He is very sensible, and he will never point it at anything that would hurt, in case it would go off accidentally. He will give a nice, sweet little dissertation on, "The Night Life of the Tsetse Fly," or "The Thrill of Coming Over the Wall in a Basket," or something else. He will leave their televisions and their rings and their bobbed hair and their worldliness alone. He will do a fancy toe dance down the aisle from one side to the other, knowing where he is going.

He will leave Sister Limberlip alone, he will not touch the Social Sallies and he will not hit at Brother Moneybags or Sister Worldly-Minded. He is very nice. He is a very genial fellow. He is a very suave personality man.

He knows how to spread the denominational wares forward and backward, right and left. He is adept at slapping backs and crossing palms in the right and proper manner. He is the hail fellow, jolly good fellow, well met.

He has been well schooled at Drip U, that he graduated from. He probably graduated at the top of his class with a *super cum laude* or some other kind of fancy handle. Came out at the head of his class Most Likely to Succeed. To prove this he is now president of the Lions Club and the Rotary Club and he is also the leading man in the Ministerial Assassination. He is a very, very successful fellow. No question about it. The professors in the college have schooled him very well in the arts of diplomacy and double talk and all the rest of the psychology, and how to treat the problems to make everybody happy and nobody sore.

Fellows like that are usually satisfied with everything except the size of their salary and length of their vacation. Lord, help us! What am I talking about? I am talking about Christ being the center or the heart of the Church.

Beautiful Ice in the Service

You can be easily fooled on Sunday morning. There is that crowd. They can sing the old songs, and everybody is saved and sanctified. Rings and all go in the air—spangles and baubles and all the rest. They have a fancy choir well covered. After all, I am for long-robed choirs. If they are going to have choirs, why not cover them up, is my philosophy.

They get up and sing and warble. Some soloist steps forward, sheared and cropped and bared, and she warbles and sings a very beautiful rendition. She really rends it from one end to the other. Tears it to shreds. You would not recognize it for a Gospel song in a month of Sundays. She turns a few fancy flip-flops and handsprings and comes sliding down the sliding board in a very gracious manner. Everybody sits there so well pleased. The ice gets deeper on the windows and thicker on the floor and the snowballs get harder in the pew and the snowman gets a little colder in the pulpit. An unconscious fellow looking around would say, "My, this church is sure going places. They have two services here on Sunday morning to accommodate the crowd. They are really going places."

They sure are. They are on their way to the hot place as fast as apostacy and indifference and carelessness and worldliness can take them.

Some church members still think that their church is a spiritual church and that Christ is the head and the heart of the church. But it is not difficult to see that that little fashionable flapper is the heart of this church. Maybe it is the pastor's wife or it could be that the preacher himself—a personality salesman—is the heart and the head of this church. Anybody with a drop of spiritual discernment could soon tell that God is 1000 miles from His temple. It takes more than stained glass windows and brick and mortar to make a church. It takes the ineffable presence of the eternal, everlasting God meeting with His people.

God in the Chickenhouse

If you are out here in a back corner somewhere worshipping in an old whitewashed chickenhouse, that chickenhouse *can* be a church. Wherever *God* is, there you will find His Church. Hallelujah.

In our own conference, few years back a young man got newly saved. The call to preach was on him, but there was no place for him to preach, for it was in the middle of the year. Fire was burning in his soul, so he went out and took over an old chickenhouse. He swept out the manure and whitewashed the walls with a brush. A few others came in to help. They boarded up the windows on the outside, put a couple of old oil stoves in there, and began to have meeting. God came, souls were saved, a church was established and the kingdom built up.

Right across the street was a fine, lofty church where the fire once fell and the glory once came, where holiness was once preached and the Bible was once taught. Now it was a habitation of bats and owls. What made the difference? The difference was God's presence—not the building, not the block, not the stone, but the presence of God!

Belt Line

I am talking about Christ, the heart of the Church. Are we on the heart line or the belt line? A good many churches are on the belt line. They say on Sunday morning, "You come back on Wednesday night or Tuesday night or Thursday night. Here on the right hand side we have a wing. In this wing we have all our recreational equipment. Here is our shuffleboard. Here is our bingo. And here is our pinochle. Here is our basketball court. Here is our athletic equipment. Here is our clubhouse over here. You can find us here on Tuesday night or Thursday night. Over here on the other side, well, this is our social activity." So, here you find them worshipping on Wednesdays and Fridays. They are bowing low at the grate where the hamburgers are fried and at the machine where the colas are poured out. The older folks are sitting around here bumping their gums and gossiping and talking. Every once in awhile you will even find a committee somewhere planning a great and momentous drive to increase the apostasy of the church by adding other blind leaders of the blind to their number.

Yes, the true heart of that church is empty. You usually find that the so-called "heart" of the church is the recreational wing and the social wing, where they eat their cake, munch their sandwiches and tell their stories. They like to indulge their appetites. They live around themselves. But despite the fact that they have a wing on the left and a wing on the right, the thing will not fly. Just will not take off. Cannot get off from the ground. Cannot rise.

I tell you, beloved friends, the holiness movement needs to do more than chuckle this morning over this picture we are drawing. It is high time we put Jesus Christ back at the heart of His church.

He is the altar. Christ is *our* altar. The prayer place, the prayer room, the fasting room. Christ should be the heart of our living. Christ should be the heart of our home. The heart! The heart!

The Dead Heart

There are preachers who wring their hands and say, "The Sunday school arm of our church and the missionary arm of our church is dying. We cannot get anybody out. We just cannot get anybody out to revival. Oh, they will come out to the Sunday school picnic or something else, but we just cannot get them out to revival, cannot get them out to prayer meeting."

I will tell you what is wrong. The heart is dead. When the heart is dead and calmed down, when the heart takes it easy and relaxes on the job, then the fingers get rather white, cold and useless, numb and dumb. The extremities begin to feel it first of all.

A lot of our churches are not dead enough yet to cover up, but they are not a long distance from a morgue. Some of our preachers are pastors of only a valley of bones. It is an amazing thing to find so many holiness churches—I mean old-fashioned churches—that are dead. Some of our churches that have a lot of high standards are dead. Some of our churches have standards, and that is all that they do have. They do not have Christ at the heart of the thing anymore. The glory is gone!

I tell you, friends, I am for the long sleeves and the long hair, but I am against a long tongue that brings a lot of deadness and lethargy, and legalism and pharisaism that kills the Spirit of God. Christ never can abide in the presence of Pharisees. I know there is another side. I know there is a liberal side. I am not for that side. But I say in very emphatic terms that unless we put more emphasis upon the life of the Master and the sacrifice of the Master and the love that comes into our life when the Master comes in, we are going to bury a lot of places that have good standards, that have high standards, and that are contending for something without the glory.

If I am misunderstood, I am misunderstood. I will tell you one thing that tries me: preachers who do not have the fortitude to point up the tremendous danger of legalism which comes unless we have a throbbing heart, a pulsating heart, a church where Christ is the heart of it all.

"These ye ought to have done, but not to have left the other undone." God help us!

4
The Hope of the Church

I WILL GIVE YOU the final thought suggested here. Christ is the *hope* of His church. Three times in this chapter the word "hope" is mentioned.

"For the hope which is laid up for you in heaven."

"The hope of the gospel which ye have held."

"And Christ in you, the hope of glory."

Hope! Hope! My friends, where would you look for hope, where would you look for a ray of light in this dark and dismal day? Would it stream out of the UN with its communistic leader and its communist sympathies? Would it come out of the White House dominated by its Roman Catholicism? Would it come out of the halls of Congress where we have hardly a statesman who is willing to put his neck on the block by speaking his mind? Would it come from denominational headquarters where they are grinding out reams of material and miles of blueprints and millions of words? Where is our hope in that direction? Is it from men? Is it in some human personality that is going to walk out on the stage of this degenerate, defying, God-hating world and sort of galvanize us together?

No. Those of us that are in the Church know that there is no hope as far as this world is concerned, or as far as human personality is concerned. *Christ is our hope!*

It is a perfect hope. He will present everyone of you perfect.

And it is a prophetic hope. It is yet to be fulfilled. Glory be to God.

It is this hope that keeps me on my feet. It is this hope that keeps me with my eyes toward the city. It is this hope that keeps me unashamed and unafraid in the midst of a wicked and perverse generation. It is this hope that keeps me with my eyes toward the city. It is this hope that keeps me unashamed and unafraid in the midst of a wicked and perverse generation. It is this hope that burns in my heart. This hope is the soon appearing of our great God and Savior, Jesus Christ.

That is the thing that keeps me from dragging my feet, from being discouraged when it comes to using my hoe in the midst of this perverse day with a long row ahead and an abundance of weeds. I can still swing the hoe. I can still preach the Gospel with fair hope of success that God Almighty one of these days is going to come. One of these days He is going to take us out of here. I am not going to whimper and cry because the row is long or because the weeds are heavy or because the hoe handle is short. I still have a glorious hope. I am going to work for His coming. I am going to wait for His coming. I am going to long for His coming. Hallelujah. He is our hope, the only real hope we have.

I am not an incurable pessimist. I am an optimist. I believe there is a way up out of this thing. Hallelujah! And that is my hope. That is what keeps the aged saints' feet from slipping out from underneath them. It is this good hope that keeps that dear old saint over there in a sickbed victorious this morning. It is this glorious hope. What is it that keeps folk with the snow of many winters upon their brows—with steps that are slow, with hands that have lost their skill, with minds that have lost their cunning—holding on? They have a hope. Glory be to God.

Why do not young people throw up their hands and quit? Why do young people prepare themselves for gospel work? Why do young people dig into their studies and pray and get a hold of their books? Because, my friend, this day is not over. Because we have a glorious hope, and we are not to be decommissioned until we hear the mighty shout from heaven.

"I must work the works of Him that sent me. The night cometh—it is on its way—but it is not here yet. So I must work the works of Him that sent me while it is day."

The Hope of Perfection

There is one aspect of this hope I like really well. It is that perfection hope—the hope I have of being perfect. Did I hear somebody laugh? I do not blame you if you did. Me, perfect? Now look at me. Me. This little old Dutchman—perfect. I could not blame anyone for breaking right out and laughing. When dear Sister Schmul thinks of me being perfect, it takes all the faith she has just to hang on. For the last almost twenty-two years she has been working on me.

I told her some time ago, "Honey, why do you bother? One of these days there is going to be a mighty shout from heaven. One of these days I am going to be perfect. Just imagine me."

That really tested her faith. That was really a hard trial for her, to imagine me being perfect. I said, "Honey, you have worked for twenty-two years and you have not got the job done, but Jesus Christ will take care of it in a moment of time and a twinkling of an eye."

Brother, it will happen like that, and there I will be perfect. Presented perfect before His throne of everlasting joy and everlasting glory. Oh, glory be to God. Oh, hallelujah!

Oh, she has got a hard row. She gets a chip now and then and she knocks off a burr here. She gets a nub off now and then, and she sort of feels rather good, but about that time something pops out in some other direction. Some oddity or idiosyncrasy begins to develop, and she has to start all over and haul me back in the same machine shop again. But, blessed be God, I have a hope one of these days. Glory be to God.

A Presentation Hope

This old Dutchman will stand in His presence. My heart has been perfect for a long time. I have made a lot of blunders on the outside, and I do not blame folks for just sort of getting the wrong idea, but my heart has been right. And one of these days, to the bottom of my soul He is going to straighten me out and fix me up as a fit subject for all eternity to enjoy His everlasting fellowship. Glory to God. That is the perfection hope I have this morning.

Do you have that kind of hope? Well, that is the only hope we have, brother, that is the only hope we have.

This is the prophetic hope. That means it is a hope that is not fulfilled yet. But it is as good as fulfilled, sir. It is as sure as that two and two make four, and then some. Oh, a prophetic hope. Do you really believe that one of these days Jesus Christ is going to give a command that is going to roll back the heavens and the sky? Then He will come tripping out of the blue. "The Lord Himself shall descend from heaven with a shout."

The Shout from Heaven

I have been thinking about that shout. I have been thinking about the voice that makes that shout. "The Lord Himself shall descend from heaven with a shout."

He is not going to send Gabriel. Oh, yes, Gabriel is going to blow his horn after awhile, but the big thing is that the Son of God is going to shout.

That shout is going to be different from any other shout. That voice is different from any other voice. John said it was like the sound of many waters. Others said it was like a multitude of voices speaking. There is a peculiar, ethereal, heavenly quality about this voice. They tried to put it down in language so that we could understand it.

Here is a voice that supersedes all the Carusos, all the Jenny Linds, and all the greatest singers. Here is a voice that supersedes them all. Not just in sound, not just in volume, but in quality.

Now notice, I said this was a personal hope. It is "Christ in you." Now get this: Christ is in every last one of us that really is in this glorious Church. "Christ is in us. Now here comes the Christ from heaven. How do you explain this, Brother Schmul?"

When Christ in heaven begins to shout, the Christ in my heart begins to answer and respond. When He says, "I come quickly," the Christ in my soul says, "Even so come quickly, Lord Jesus."

Something begins now to tremble in my soul—hallelujah—Just in anticipation of hearing that glorious shout.

We have a little organ in our home. My eldest son said the other day, "Daddy, come over here and listen. I want you to notice what happens when I set these bass keys and put this bass pedal on."

So I went over and he put the bass on real heavy. He said, "Now watch, Dad, over there on the window sill." My wife has a little figurine with a cracked head, one of these kinds that wiggle and bobble back and forth. He said, "Now watch, Dad."

He began to play a gospel song heavy on the bass and that little old thing began to wiggle and to dance, and something hit my heart. I said, "Oh, God, that is exactly what is going to happen one of these days."

When that peculiar voice is heard on that celestial wavelength, something is going to begin to move. Something is going to begin to change in my soul. Hallelujah. When Jesus Christ speaks, when He shouts that glorious shout, something is going to happen in the dust of the earth. The dormitories of the dead are going to open up wide. The doors of the cave where Abraham, Isaac, Jacob and the rest are buried in Mizpeh are going to swing open wide. Here come Abraham, Isaac and Jacob all walking out. Why? They hear the voice. They are moved by the power of that voice, and out of the dust they come. Out of the dormitories of the dead they arise, on marching, triumphant feet. Oh, they hear the glorious voice of the triumphant Son of God. That is our hope.

Who is This?

In the Song of Solomon, there are three questions raised. Who is this that cometh out of the wilderness like pillars of smoke, perfume with myrrh and frankincense and with all the powder of the merchant? Who is this? It is Christ, coming in His greatness, His stature, His beauty, His plenitude, His omnipotence. Here He comes. He is on His way.

Another question: Who is she that looketh forth as the morning, fair as the moon, clear as the sun, and terrible as an army with banners? Who is that? That is the Church. Hallelujah. There she is. Robed for battle, sword in her hand, spear by her side, helmet upon her head, feet shod, here she is.

Once again divine inspiration says, "Who is this that cometh up from the wilderness, leaning upon her beloved?" Who is this? It is you and I. It is this glorious Church. And where is she coming from? She is coming out of the wilderness. That is this world. This world is a wilderness. It is a cursed world of thieves and thistles and briars. It is a jungle world. It is a wild world. But here we are coming. Hallelujah!

We have heard His voice. He comes in the greatness of His strength. He comes with the pillars of His power. He comes with all the perfumes of the merchant. Here He comes and here we are. We are not walking with our chests out and our heads high. No, sir. Here we come leaning on the arm of our beloved.

The battles are over. The conflict is ended. That is in the past. Here I come out. Blessed be God. He is going to get every last one of us out of this wilderness. He is going to take every last one out of this cursed world. This deliverance is for those who come, leaning on His arm.

I want to make this confession; I say it sincerely from my heart: I cannot get out of this world alone. I cannot make it through the wilderness alone. I would be confused and muddled. There are so many voices and so many confusing circumstances and situations, I could not get out of it alone. I would not trust my brethren as much, as I love and appreciate them.

No, I would not trust a soul. I must lean on the arm of my beloved. If I am going to get out of here, if I am going to make heaven my home, I must confess my weaknesses, I must confess my limitations, I must confess my poverty, I must lean on His arm. And He has guaranteed to take me out. Hallelujah for Jesus! I am glad I am a member of that Church. Are you?

We love Thee, Jesus. Thou art the head of the Church. Thou art the heart of the Church. Thou art the hope of the Church. We love Thee. We adore Thee. We confess our weaknesses. We confess our limitations. Thou wilt bring us out, glory be to God.

PART II
LET ME SEE THE KING'S FACE

5

The Difference Between Christians

"Let me see the King's face" (II Samuel 14:32).

THIS IS THE STORY of Absalom, who spent three years in exile after he had slain his brother, Amnon, who had defiled his sister, Tamar. You perhaps remember the interesting story of the woman of Tekoah that came before King David and pled in disguise through a parable until the eyes of the king were opened and he granted permission for Absalom to come back from Gershur and live in the king's city, which was Jerusalem.

After he was brought back to the city, according to our lesson today, Absalom spent two years without yet seeing the king. These two years on top of the three years he had spent in exile, added up to five years altogether that he had not seen his father's face. This meant that he had not seen the king's face, for David was his father.

During those two years in the same town, perhaps in sight of his father's palace, he waited for an invitation to go and see his father. Absalom was getting considerably distressed. After all, he was the king's son. After all, the king had invited him to come back to the city. After all, he felt he did have some rights. But he had not been invited in to see the king even though he had made once again an approach through his good friend, Joab, who saw the king probably almost everyday. Joab had paid little or no attention, or else had no success. Now, since Absalom was unable to get his message through, he hit upon a plan whereby he might really impress upon Joab's mind that he insisted on seeing the king. He said to a servant, "See, Joab's barley field is right next to mine. Go out there and set his field on fire. Maybe that will get his attention."

When Joab saw the smoke arising in his barley field—I do not know how he was dressed, or whether it was morning or late at night—he came out, ready or unready, and said, "What is going on here, and what do you want?"

Absalom did have a way of getting people's attention. He said, "Look, I have stayed in this town two years. It has been five years altogether since I have seen the king's face. Now, the king apparently has forgiven me because he called me back home. Let me see the king's face. And if there is any iniquity in me, let him slay me. But I am refusing to stay here if I cannot see the king's face. I might as well have stayed in Gershur. I was just as well off in exile a long way off, as I am to live here in Jerusalem, if I cannot see the king's face."

Now the point is that there is a difference between just Christians and a Christian. The difference that has distinguished a Christian from other Christians across the centuries—in his writings, in his testimony, and in his life—has been the passion, "Let me see the king's face." This is the thing that has distinguished that one. This is the thing that separates good Christians from the best. This is the distinguishing line—his passion. "I refuse to just live in the king's town; or to be the king's deliveryman; or to curry the king's horses; or to run on the king's errands; or to polish the kings chariot; or to serve at the king's table. I want to see the king. Let me see His face."

Samuel Rutherford said, "One smile from the Christ's face is to me as the kingdom." Murray McCheyne said, "No amount of activity in the King's business makes up for neglect of the King." Fellowship with the King and beholding His face carries its own reward. I am afraid there have been times when I have been content to run errands and polish a chariot and even carry water for His Elijahs, but I have not seen him. The complications that have come in my own spiritual life and existence have come because I have been satisfied with lesser things instead of pressing my claim to see the King—to see His face.

When Oswald Chambers was in Egypt working with the troops during World War I, a skeptical English schoolteacher was in the YMCA lobby one day. She turned to a friend and said, "Who is that man over there?" She motioned toward a tall, gangling-looking fellow. "Who is that fellow?"

"Why," they said, "that is Mr. Chambers. He is working with the YMCA. He is a minister."

"I have never seen a face like that," she said. "That face looks like the face of Jesus."

She was a skeptic, claimed to be an agnostic, but one look at the face of Oswald Chambers knocked all of her skepticism and agnosticism out of her. She became a devout Christian because she had looked in the face of a man who lived in the face of the Son of God.

As I look over the Bible there are some characters that stand out brighter and taller than all the rest. The reason they do is because they were men and women that were not satisfied with just working about the King's business, keeping busy in the King's work and being the King's chore boy, but they were souls who occasionally laid aside their chore rags and their polishing cloths, laid aside their curry combs and their brushes, and just made it their business to see the King Himself.

Anyone Can See the King's Face

You know, the thing that thrills me is that even a chore boy, or a scullery girl, or one from the kitchen can lay these things aside and go to see the King. One does not have to be a DD or a theological giant to see the King. Anybody can go in and see the King, if he is a son.

You can go in. You may have got into trouble and have gone into exile for awhile because you made a blunder. You can still come back home, and because you are a son, you have a right to demand to see the King's face.

I am glad we have a King that does not exile us just because we stumble and make a colloquial bungle. Here is a King who has not closed the doors. David was a great king, but here is the King of kings. Here is Jesus, into whose presence we all can come, and should come. Let us just lay aside our scullery cloths and brushes and make today the day when we are going to see the King's face.

Esther

When Esther came into the King's presence, she was not sure of the reception she was going to get. She said, "If he slays me, he slays me. If I perish, I perish."

But, my friend, here is a King who has opened wide the doors and who has extended, as it were, the golden sceptre of divine promise. It is before me today. And if there be any iniquity in me when I see His face I can beg His pardon. I can plead His blood. I can ask for His atonement. I can find balm for my healing. I can find grace for my soul. "Let me see the king's face today, and I shall be satisfied."

6
Moses the Incomparable

MOSES WAS A MAN who insisted on seeing His face. Moses was *incomparable*. Oh, how few characters, in the Old or New Testament, can be compared with Moses. What made Moses such an incomparable character? Well, he had an incomparable anger spring from a holy jealousy because of his love for God.

When he stood on the glorious mount for six days there were times of great silence. For six days there was no voice. For six days there was no one in sight. But for six days there was the blessed presence of God. On the seventh day God spoke. The Commandments were given. Moses lingered for forty days, and the people became rather nervous and jittery, as people are wont to become when they are unaccustomed to divine presence, when they are unaware of divine interactions that are going on not very far away. It is amazing how quickly we get caught up in other things when our minds and our thoughts are afar off from spiritual and eternal things.

When Moses came down from the Mount he heard singing, he heard music, and he heard the people dancing and shouting, having a high time. But when he saw the golden calf something within him stirred: anger—holy, pure anger. Jealousy for God and for His glory manifested itself in his soul. He had lived in the blessed presence of the ineffable face of God. And now when he came down and saw this dead, materialistic idol that had taken the place of the true and living God, he broke their image to pieces. He ground it to powder, and then he made them drink the brackish waters of their own sin and of their own rebellion. This was a holy jealousy, a holy anger.

A capacity for righteous indignation for the honor of God has invariably characterized those who have insisted on seeing the King's face. Brother, we do need this today. Why is it we tolerate so much and permit so much that is contrary to God and righteousness and holiness? Because we are so little conscious of His presence and live so little in His glory. How enticing and intriguing and mysterious sin becomes when we live away from that face.

I look at my own experience—the times when I have almost failed, the times when I faltered in my purpose. It has been when I was living too long out of the presence of that face. It has been when I was too busy darting about on the King's business and running the King's errands—making a mimeograph machine turn perhaps, or visiting other members of the King's family. I got so busy here and there that I neglected visiting the King and seeing the King's face. I got interested in earthly things and, oh, the things of eternity fade away when I get engrossed in the earthly and material things. But when I insist and say, "Let me see the King's face today," all things else begin to fall into their right places, and I begin to see how small and insignificant they are. A holy jealousy for God's honor and for God's cause and for God's glory covers my soul, inspires my heart and puts a fierceness in my being for the honor of God, for the standards of God, for the purity of His worship, for the holiness of His message and for the glory of His power and presence.

And I remember in my early ministry—and I think I can say that now, because I have been preaching almost thirty years—I can remember how that as a young preacher I reasoned as to what way I would take. I wanted to be a success. I wanted to make a mark. I wanted to excel. I wanted to put the little church I had on the map. I saw it all in relation to God's work, and "this is doing something for God." I saw the short cuts that were necessary if I would make such a goal. I saw the detours that were necessary if I would arrive at such a goal. I had men that were well-versed that told me what I could do. They told me of talents either seen or unseen, they thought of me as possessing, and many other things. And I almost missed it.

I will never forget the day when I came into the presence of the King, and these things began to fall down like tenpins. They began to tumble over like the little lead soldiers they were—the tinseling toys, the big churches, the lofty offices, the high places that they said that could be mine if I only would. They just fell into place when I saw the King's face. When I came out of the place, I can say to the glory of God, there has never been any deviation, though I have been called everything in the catalog. There has never been any deviation in my soul. I see things as they are in the light of eternity—that vision is clear. That holy jealousy for God's cause and for His honor and for His glory burns brightly as long as I keep the King's face in full view. It is then that these things take on their proper proportions.

An Increasing Appetite

Moses was not only comparable in the holy jealousy and godly anger that brought him to a complete and perfect loyalty to God, but he had an incomparable hunger. Though he had spent forty days and forty nights in a mountain that thundered with the thunders of God and flashed with the effervescent lightnings from the throne of the eternal; though he had stood on the mountain that did exceedingly quake and thunder and rock and roll; though he had stood for six days in the blazing perfections of God; yet just a few days after he said, "Show me thy glory."

He had an incomparable hunger. He never seemed to be satisfied, never seemed to be content. He was forty days in such splendor; forty days in such glory; forty days in the presence of such mighty power. But here he was, pleading, "Show me thy glory. Show me thy glory."

This attitude invariably characterizes those that live in the presence of that blessed face. Those that would say, "Let us see the King's face," invariably evidence a continuing appetite and hunger for the glory of God. They never weary of it. They never tire of it. They are never satiated by it. There is an insatiable appetite in their souls that cries, "Show me more. Show me thy glory." Amen.

These people are always drinking but always thirsty. They are always feeding, but they are always empty. They talk about being full, but they are always pulling their chairs up for another round. They are always being satisfied, but they are always asking for more heavenly manna.

Did you ever feed a hungry teenaged boy? Did you ever watch the silo of pancakes disappear almost miraculously, to be replaced by another stack? There they are, but now they, too, are disappearing. You look at the lad in amazement and wonder. And if you have two or three of those empty stomachs around, brother, you wonder if you are not going to have to float a loan before long to keep the whole business solid and keep the table supplied. It is a gallon of syrup and another stack.

We had a couple of young fellows at our church a few days back, and one of the ladies of the church brought in a large package of biscuits. And she said, "Here is something to help out at the parsonage." I said, "Sister, these two boys can inhale more of those accidentally than the rest of our family can eat on purpose." Well, that is about it. That is a wonderful experience, and that is a wonderful appetite.

Moses had that kind of an appetite. Brother, he pulled his chair up and dined on the dainties of heaven for forty days and forty nights. Every shelf in God's pantry, with all the blessed things his soul required, was down where he could get into it but as soon as he took his napkin and wiped his lips he said, "Show me now thy glory."

This invariably characterizes those that have the cry in their souls, "Let me see the King's face."

Archangels will not Suffice

Then Moses had an incomparable concern for God's way as well as for God's presence. In the book of Exodus the Lord said, "Now I will send an angel before thee."

But Moses was not satisfied with this. He said, "Well, an angel may be all right, Lord, but as far as I am concerned, if Thou art not going to carry us up hence, we are not going. If thy presence carry us not up hence, we are not going. I appreciate angels, Father. I know Gabriel is a very capable being. I know Michael is a very powerful being. I know all of the other angels you have are worthy, obedient messengers, but I am not interested in angels for companions. I am not interested in archangels for fellowship. I am not interested in their might or in their power. It is your presence I want, Lord, and if your presence go not with us, then do not carry us up. Lord, I would rather die here. Let us bleach our bones here rather than go one step of the way without you, Lord, without your very own divine and glorious presence."

Say, is that how you feel about it? If you live in the presence of His face, if you put your junk down long enough to go into His presence and talk with the King face to face, brother, you will not be satisfied with a substitute. You will not be satisfied with any other way, whether it be an angel or whether it be your superior in the church that says, "Now this is the way."

If God is not taking that way—though all the rest of the church is going that way—if God is not taking that way, you will turn your back on it and go the way God is leading you to go. Amen. Yes, "if thy presence go not with us, then carry us not up hence."

His Way, His Will

Further, God's presence means that the way we are taking is His will. It is His way. His presence is an assurance of grace for the journey no matter how dark the night or how hot the day, or how windy the desert, or how rugged the mountains.

"We will not mind the travel as long as Thy presence goes with us. Lord, we will not fuss about the mountains high or the desert drear or about the blackness of the night. We will not fuss about the fare or contend about what we have to eat on the way. If Thou wilt go with us we care not whether there are wells there or springs there or oases there or men or meat there. We will not fuss about anything if Thy presence is there. Thy presence will make our Paradise. Thy presence is our souls' holy and glorious delight." Glory be to God.

7
Paul the Inexhaustible

TURN TO THE WRITINGS of the Apostle Paul. I am amazed at what was crowded into his life—the whippings, the shipwrecks, the imprisonments; the stripes; the preachings, the prayings, the fastings; the writings, the long journeys, the tedious hours; the times of imprisonment, the misunderstandings, the misrepresentations. And yet, one never finds the Apostle Paul taking it easy or settling down or merely fanning himself under a pomegranate tree as we do Saul in the Old Testament. He is always going. He is always doing. He is always praying. He is always writing. It almost makes a person weary and tired to read of all his exploits and escapades and adventures.

Now, he is riding around in a boat in the Mediterranean. It is held together with haybale wire and binder twine. He and his companions have not seen the light of the sun or the moon or the stars for at least two weeks. They have hit a mighty storm called Euroclydon. The thunders have rolled overhead. The piercing lightening has punctured the sky. The canvas—what is left of it—hangs in tatters. The mainmast is down. Nobody can eat. Everybody is sick. The upper decks and the lower decks have been awash for days. But at last this man stands out and says, "Sirs, be of good cheer."

The next thing we find he is floating around on a chunk of spar somewhere out in the middle of the same sea.

What is the Source of Such Strength?

If he is not being tossed about in the Mediterranean, he is being pelted with rocks by the scribes or by the pharisees. And if he is not on a boat riding or being pelted with rocks, he is shaking a serpent into a red hot fire someplace. If he is not shaking a serpent into a fire, he is sitting in prison writing laboriously an epistle to the Galatians or to somebody else. He is rousing them or stirring them or poking at their spiritual pride or working on their lethargy or rousing and prodding them to greater exploits of God.

If he is not writing he is riding over wall in a basket, getting out of the city just in the nick of time. And on top of all this, he pastors groups of folk here and there—wrestles with the carnal Corinthians and instructs the pious Ephesians. He is everlastingly working. He is an inexhaustible character.

Where did he find his reservoirs? How did this little beat-up follower of Jesus (about four foot eleven inches) get all of his energy? Where did he find his inspiration? Did he find it in a camp meeting somewhere? Or in a holiness convention? Or in reading somebody else's pious writings? No, no, no! He found it because everlastingly he looked into the King's face. Hallelujah!

He was not so busy with his ear to the ground trying to find out what the current system was or what the political moves were in the church at Jerusalem that he did not have time to see the King. He was not even worried about what Jerusalem was doing. He said, "I went up to Jerusalem to those that seemed to be somewhat." And I rather like that phrase. That is quite typical at least of things in our day. "To those who seem to be somewhat." He went up to headquarters. But he said, "They did not add anything to me."

This was because one day he had met Jesus Christ on the road to Damascus, and from that day on he maintained a full view of the glorious face of the Blessed Redeemer, Jesus Christ. The carnal Corinthians thought he was beside himself. They were sure he was a little bit "tetched," especially when he thought he was some kind of an ambassador. He did not look like an ambassador. He did not have the appearance of an ambassador or the fancy little "show-er" instead of a "blower" in his pocket. He did not have any of the other credentials of an ambassador.

He was always going. He was always writing. He was always fighting. He was always going to jail or getting out of jail. He was always in some kind of a revival or a riot or a scrap. He was either up or he was down, but he said, "In whatsoever state I am, I have learned to be therewith content." Glory be to God!

The Face on the Damascus Road

Well, where does he get his strength for it all? He is drawing strength from the face of Jesus Christ whom he beheld on the road to Damascus. And he kept that face before him, not only that day, but every moment of every day that succeeded that. And there is the source of his spiritual perpetual motion. Such people are going night and day everlastingly for God. Amen.

This passion for Christ did something for the Apostle. It kept him sweet in the midst of controversy. When Jerusalem had their councils and they debated and they talked and they discussed a lot of things concerning this and that, the apostle kept sweet about it. And on down the road he goes to the next preaching mission.

It seems to me that it was almost a trial for the apostle to go to the general conference or the business meeting and go through all that kind of stuff. It seems as though he could not get out of town soon enough to get to the first preaching station. To get out to the first place where he could begin to expound the glorious wonders of redeeming grace and to tell the blessed story. But it is this that kept him sweet in the midst of controversy.

He said, "I withstood Peter to his face because he was to be blamed." Brother, let us not kid ourselves, if you think you are going to go through the world without controversy. If you think you are going to get anything done for God, you are going to be a controversial figure. You are going to be a controversial personality.

Keeping Sweet in Controversy

Robb French opened up a camp meeting and a school in Florida, and I heard sometime back he was running a gas station out here on Route 1 somewhere. Other folks talk about "how much money he is worth."

Somebody said the other day that Glenn Griffith has a motel that is half a mile long, and "he owns a very wonderful and valuable property there." That is another big lie.

But after all, if you do anything for God you are bound to have people tell lies. You are bound to be a center of controversy. But in the midst of it all the Apostle Paul was as sweet as heaven. The Apostle Paul kept his equilibrium. What did it? He kept his eyes on the face of Jesus Christ.

I am here to tell you something, brother. There is something more important than winning an argument, and that is maintaining the right spirit and maintaining a right attitude. The greatest liability the old-fashioned crowd has to carry around is the liability we have to carry. We do not have grace to overlook anybody else's faults. We do not have any extra grace to forgive or to look with charity upon a brother. We do not have room in our heart unless he stands perfectly straight and sets up here just so. We do not have room for him.

Brother, if you had an enlargement of heart that comes by looking in the full and open face of Jesus Christ, you would have room in your heart to stand them all and to put them in crosswise—to bring them in with all their prejudices. You would still have room for them in your own heart if you live in the glorious light of His beautiful face.

Yes, he kept sweet in the middle of the controversy. He kept straight on his course for Christ without either being legal or liberal. He did not fall in one hand or fall in the other. Brother, that is a big job: to keep sweet and stand for holiness. And here is where this love comes in again.

Setting a Straight Course

This is the thing that kept Paul straight on his course. He saw Christ in His glory and the powers and the privileges that are in Jesus Christ, and he steered a straight course toward the Celestial City. If you look to the right or if you look to the left you are going to get into trouble. If you try to follow somebody over here or follow somebody over there, just staggering from one side of the road to the other, you are going to be cross-eyed and knock-kneed and pigeon-toed, and you are going to wind up in hell to boot.

I am not interested in trying to find the middle of the road. I do not have any time for that expression. But I am interested in keeping my face and my eyes on Jesus Christ. If you keep your eyes on Jesus Christ you are going to find out you are in the center of the will of God.

And you will not find the face of Jesus Christ in left field or right field. You will find the face of Jesus Christ in the perfect center of the will of God. Then, if you will stay in the perfect center of the will of God, where you can see that face, you will have love for the fellow on the right, you will have love for the fellow on the left, and you will have love that covers and uncovers a multitude of sins.

I get kicked from folks on both sides of the road, and that is how I know I am in the middle. Some say, "Well, you have gone too far." A lot of others say, "You have not gone far enough." I am not concerned about what you think where I have gone. I am concerned where I am going. The only way I know that I will not miss the way is to keep my eyes on Jesus Christ who is the *center* of the way—who is the *heart* of the way; who is the *life* of the way; who is the *glory* of the way; who is the *inspiration* for the way. Glory be to God! Brother, that is almost enough to make a Wesleyan Methodist shout, and that takes a lot.

This kept Paul steadfast amidst hostile circumstances; this kept him submissive to the will of Christ—this looking in the face of Jesus Christ. This holding the face of Jesus Christ always before him is what kept him standing on the tiptoe expectancy for the exit sign to come on when he would hear the call, "Come up higher."

Brother, keep your eyes on Jesus and you will be standing on tiptoe expectancy. Look into His face day by day. Keep the glorious, beautiful, illustrious, unique and shining face in your gaze, and you will be standing on tiptoe expectancy looking for the glorious appearing of our Lord and Savior, Jesus Christ.

8
Mary the Indomitable

YES, MARY, OUT OF whom Jesus cast seven devils. Mary, who was undismayed. Mary, who would not be discouraged. Mary, who would not give up. The Mary who would not say "die." Mary, the Indomitable. The Mary who seemed intuitively and instinctively to do the thing that pleased the Master. This Mary who was transformed—this Mary who had been so gloriously delivered—is an outstanding example of one who kept the face of Jesus Christ before her.

Note her devotion and her courage and the steadfastness and her love. It was this instinctive love within her that caused her to bathe the Master's feet and to wipe them with her tresses of golden hair. It was this love and this devotion for Christ and Christ alone that moved her to lavish on Him her rarest treasure, when other disciples turned a cold stare and said, "Why was this waste made?" When others were cold and indifferent, her devotion—her devotion to her Christ, her devotion to her Redeemer, her devotion to her Lord, her devotion to her King—this is what led her to break that precious box. When others could see no cause for sacrifice, could not recognize a special occasion, Jesus said, "She hath done it for my burial."

She did not understand all that the Master was involved in this thing. She did not understand the theology. She did not understand the doctrine. But in her heart something spoke to her. In her soul something talked to her.

It was this Mary that stood by the cross. She was not big enough to fight a legion. She was not big enough to push away a centurion. But she was big enough to stay after all the disciples had walked away and had forsaken Him and fled. She was still lingering when the darkened shadows were falling across the Judean hills and the pall of blackness had spread over the countryside, and the three crosses were pointing towards heaven. Even after she heard Him cry, "It is finished," and after He gave up the ghost, she lingered. She stayed. Her indomitable courage! Her love! Her devotion! She was clinging to Him, and only when they took Him down did she follow them to where they would lay Him, that she might be sure where He was placed. Only then would she retire. The others had left. The others had gone their way.

It was this same love, this indomitable spirit, this courage and devotion to Christ that led her to the sepulchre before the chariot of the sun began to rise on that Easter morning, long before the silver shafts of light began to penetrate the eastern hills. She was there before the first glimmer was seen. She was there before the first light was kindled. The lights of the stars, still sprinkled brightly overhead, found her lingering there. Her beloved was there. The One she loved was there. She had not understood when others said, "We had hoped." She still had hope. When others had walked away she still stood by. When others had given up in despair she clung tenaciously on, glory to God.

Why? She had seen His face. That day when she looked in His face, He looked in her face and saw one that was demon possessed and demon filled. It was then that the gracious spirit of the Son of God was exercised upon that demented mind and that wretched and depraved soul. When He looked upon her and cast out the seven devils and transformed her, she saw something in that look that she never got away from, that she never could shake, that she never could let pass away.

And so early in the morning she was there among the lilies and among the flowers. She was waiting. Her faith was there. Her confidence was still there.

High IQ Not Required

What brought her there? Not her logic. Not reason brought her there. She did not understand the intricacies of this thing. She did not understand the judgment of God and the mercies of God and the atonements and the sacrifices. She was not familiar with the doctrine of the atonement, with all of the difficulties involved in man's redemption.

But intuitively something in her heart told her something. And while her head could not reason and her mind could not explain, while hell may have tortured because she could not understand and may have made light of her because of her love and devotion, yet the vision of that face in her heart and in her own mind brought her, in love and devotion, early on this morning.

Well, she was not disappointed.

You know, I am just a dumb fellow. I really do not know very much. And when this came to me that Mary loved and gave though she could not understand, it just did something for my little old dumb, Dutch head, and it did something for my heart. Praise God! Brother, I just cannot explain a lot of things. I do not know a lot of things about God or about redemption or about suffering or about heartache or about sorrow. I do not understand them. I am just frank to tell you I do not. But I know this.

Job did not understand them all, but he said, "Though He slay me I am going to trust Him." There is something in the heart of a fellow, there is something in the heart of a woman, that if they will really look full in the face of Jesus Christ and keep a steadfast gaze there, there is something in that heart that, though they cannot understand, though they cannot comprehend, though they cannot make explanation that would satisfy an atheist, or even make an explanation that would satisfy another member of the family, or cannot make an explanation that would satisfy even another child of God, somehow or another in their heart it has been resolved and they accepted it and they understand it in a way that no man can explain. They understand it. They believe it. They really own it. They stretch themselves out on it and find glorious rest and glorious peace. And such souls are never disappointed. Brother, in the midst of confessing your ignorance and all, you will have a glorious revelation. Hallelujah!

The Face in the Dark

This morning while Mary was there, the darkness hovering over, a figure appeared. "It must be the gardener," she thought. Oh, how our eyes are holden at times that we cannot see! "It must be the gardener." And then she had a reward that would satisfy anybody. She heard her own name fall from the lips of the Master. "Mary."

Does a name over sound more sweet than it sounds when it is spoken by your mother or by your sweetheart? No, only when it is spoken by the Master. "Mary."

Suddenly something happened. Something happened inside. "I thought it was the gardener," she confessed. Then she cried, "Rabboni! Oh, why did I not recognize Him? Why did I not know it was He? Why did I not?"

Well, sufficient that He was there. Yes, she beheld His face. She now fell at His feet. She would lay hold upon Him so as to never let Him go. But the Master restrained her.

"Not now, Mary. I have not ascended, yet. But I have a message. You have been such a faithful servant…"

Brother, here is the greatest sermon ever preached. I have heard some great sermons, but this is the greatest sermon out of Jesus Christ that anybody ever preached. "Mary," He commissioned her, "I want you to preach a sermon. Go to my disciples, and especially go to Peter."

"And Peter." Oh! That does something to me, for I am so much like Peter. So many time I have faltered in my devotions. So many times I have slipped away when I should have stood by. So many times my gaze has been attracted by other things, and I have sort of wandered off. I was not there when I should have been there. I was not staying by faithfully. It got dark and other people deserted, other people left, other folks went their way, and I sort of felt, "The other fellows are all wandering out. I will go, too." Sometimes it has happened in prayer meeting. Sometimes it has happened in camp meeting. Sometimes it has happened in life in general. I have sort of wandered out. Then, after I have gone, I have heard some lonely soul wrestled with God until heaven came down, his soul to greet, and when he came and told me about it I felt like Peter must have felt when Mary said, "Peter, He is risen! He is risen!"

Oh, I am glad for one thing. Old Peter had the run in his feet. He took to his heels right away. "If that is so," we hear him say, "I am going back where He is. I am heading back in the right direction. I am making tracks for His presence. I am sorry…"

My dear friend, I tell you how I feel in my soul: let me see the King's face today! It shall be my meat and drink. Oh, that I might see the King's face today!

Let us, in our own way, press our way through until we can all see His face. We need to have outpouring, but how can we get it unless we get into His presence?

Part III
Living Like the Master

9
The Greatest Trials Come From our Brethren

Luke 6

I WOULD LIKE TO talk to you, if the Lord might help us, from the thought suggested here in verse forty, "Living Like the Master." I think this is the highest ambition I have—to live like Jesus. I desire this more than anything else. I truly and sincerely desire to live like the Master.

Mahatma Gandhi on one occasion said, "I would be a Christian if it were not for the Christians."

We are called Christians because we are to be Christ-like. The Bible makes it clear that the perfection spoken of in Luke 6:40, "everyone that is perfect," is a moral perfection—not a perfection of the head, or of the hand, but a perfection of the heart. I found out a long time ago that when your head gets you into trouble, if you have this perfection, the Lord drops a long-play record on your heart which begins, "Fix it up, fix it up, fix it up." That tune is played with monotonous regularity until you fix it up. Otherwise, the song birds will forever quit singing in your heart.

Sad to say, much of the time of the present-day followers of Jesus Christ is spent defending their bad tempers and sour dispositions and unchrist-like attitudes. Once again I believe we could say that there would be a lot more Christians in the world today if it were not for the "Christian."

Now there is one lesson made clear in the Book and that lesson is before us. That lesson is that the grace of holiness is to be so manifested in our lives that whether it be the crucible of misunderstanding or misrepresentation that troubles us, whether it be lies or evil speaking or evil report by false brethren, whether the suffering come from within or without, the life of Jesus is to be made in our mortal bodies.

Jesus received His most unkind and telling blows from those within, not from those without. Not from the outsiders, but from the insiders. Not from the Romans necessarily, but from the Jews of His own fellowship. The Master's greatest source of trouble came from members of His own family that doubted Him—his own brothers that did not believe Him, those that carried a question mark concerning His divinity, concerning His life, concerning His ministry. His greatest source of trial, of discomfort, of wakeful hours and of rolling and tossing at night came from disciples that later forsook Him and denied Him. Eventually, one sold Him.

And so we find that as Christians, we need not be surprised if the source of our own greatest discomfort and irritation comes, not from without, but from those within.

Living According to the Law of Our Nature

Now, this sixth chapter of Like reveals that there is a divine nature and that there is depraved nature and that we all live according to the law of our natures.

If you will notice this chapter carefully you will see that there is a natural division beginning with verse twenty. There we have the profile of a disciple by way of contrast. "Blessed, blessed, blessed are the poor and the meek and the merciful, etc."

Then, beginning with verse twenty-seven we have the delineation of the divine nature. The divine nature is identified by the words, "Love," "Bless," "Pray," "Give thy cloak," "Merciful," "Love thine enemies," "Be ye kind to the unthankful," "Be ye merciful as your Father in heaven is also merciful," "Judge not," "Condemn not," and "Give."

These words are all typical of the divine nature, and they are typical of those that have the divine nature. Christians are easily identified by this characterization. This message came early in the ministry of the Master. It came while He was preaching to His disciples within the hearing of a great multitude. It is known as "The Sermon on the Mount."

Actually, what Jesus is saying to the people on the outer fringes who are listening to this message is, "This is how you are going to be able to distinguish my disciples. They will have a different nature. These words will characterize them wherever they may be found, and everyone that is perfect shall be as his Master."

Then He makes it clear that there is a depraved nature and no matter how much these disciples may testify to something else, Jesus is saying here, "You can identify a person that is depraved no matter if he professes to be my disciple. Everyone that is perfect is going to be like me. I am going to give you a pattern. This is the pattern that my disciples shall live by. You will not have any trouble discovering or defining my disciples, for every disciple is going to be true to his nature. Of thorns men do not gather figs and of a bramble mush men do not gather grapes. A good tree brings forth good fruit, and an evil tree brings forth evil fruit. You can tell my disciples by their fruit. From the abundance of their hearts their mouths will speak."

Blind Optometrists

Jesus makes it very clear that the depraved disciple is recognized by the fact that he loves those that love him. He makes it very clear in verse thirty-two and repeats it two or three times that if we love those that love us, no grace at all is involved. Any person with any measure of sense at all will certainly play up to the person that plays up to him. If we merely love the people that love us and flatter our ego, that pamper our pride, that overlook our weaknesses as we overlook theirs, if we sort of embrace a mutual admiration society, there is no grace involved. So He makes it clear at the very beginning that a depraved individual will love those that love him.

Then Christ goes on to say that you can identify these depraved disciples by the fact that they are hypercritical. They are very critical about other people. They are everlastingly hunting for sawdust in someone else's eye, but they are neglecting the weightier matters of the law so far as they themselves are concerned. And they are blind. Their own eyes are filled with sawlogs while they are out busy trying to locate some sawdust in somebody else's eyes.

If I were going to an optometrist, I certainly would not go to a blind one. If I need an operation on my eyes I want a doctor who has two good eyes of his own with which he can see clearly, and I would prefer a doctor who does not wear glasses, if possible.

There are a lot of blind dummies around the country today that are everlastingly probing. They are blind leaders of the blind. They are putting out more eyes, driving more people into the ditch, driving more folks away from God and righteousness and holiness by their moat-hunting and their sin-sniffing than they are helping.

Once again we can say that we would be Christians if it were not for the Christians. God help us every one.

Jesus said, "It hath been said of old time an eye for an eye and a tooth for a tooth and a wound for a wound and a stripe for a stripe. But I say unto you in this new day, in this new dispensation, it shall not be so with my disciples. And those of you that are out on the outer fringe listening to this Olivet discourse today, here is how you can tell my disciples. Everyone that is perfect shall be in profile as I am. He shall be as his Master."

Now, how are we going to explain that away? What are we going to do with this Scripture?

As I said before, one of the popular pastimes in holiness crowds is everlastingly defending our bad tempers and sour dispositions and our unchrist-like attitudes—everlastingly making excuses for one thing or another. But I want you to notice that the scripture teaches very clearly and very plainly that you and I are to live like the Master. And if you are not living like the Master in the area of your nature, if your disposition is not saturated with the divine Personality, if you are not a true partaker of the divine nature, sooner or later your true nature will come to light.

Do They See the Son Revealed in Me?

You can attend camp meeting and shout and then go out and fail to pay your bills and be difficult to get along with if somebody does not look after you and pamper you and love you. Your true nature sooner or later will come to light.

The Bible teaches emphatically that the divine disposition, the divine nature, is to be implanted in your heart by the Holy Ghost, and that everyone that is perfect is as his Master.

Now notice what Paul says in Galatians 1:15-16: "But it pleased God to reveal His Son in me." Now, my dear friend, that is a tremendous statement. "It pleased God to reveal His Son in me." Think of God revealing His Son in you and in me. Think of that. Do you really transmit a proper image of the Son to the world? Or could it be said of you and me in our fellowship and in our communities and among our relatives whom we are so anxiously hoping to see saved, "I would be a Christian if it were not for my brother-in-law or my mother-in-law or my father-in-law, or my son or my daughter, or someone else." Put whosoever's name you want to in there, who claims to be a Christian.

Do they see the Son revealed in me?

10
Earthen Vessels?

Now turn over if you will to II Corinthians 4 and begin to read with verse seven: "But we have this treasure in earthen vessels that the excellency of the power may be of God and not of us."

I have heard some preach on this text to show us how human we are and to make all kinds of room and excuses for weaknesses and nerves and one thing and another. And that is right and legitimate. They are stressing the fact that we have this treasure in earthen vessels. We do have this treasure in earthen vessels, but let us not stop there. Let us read the rest of this section: "We are troubled on every side, yet not distressed; we are perplexed, but not in despair; persecuted, but not forsaken; cast down, but not destroyed; always bearing about in the body the dying of the Lord Jesus, that the life also of Jesus might be made manifest in our body."

Now please notice the repetition of this phrase in the next two verses. "That the life also of Jesus might be made manifest in our body." Then he repeats it just in case you might have missed it: "We which are alive are always delivered unto death for Jesus' sake that the life also of Jesus might be made manifest in our mortal flesh."

We are everlastingly excusing our glibness and our harshness and our wrong attitudes and our wrong dispositions and our bad tempers and our sour dispositions or blaming them on our grandfathers or our Dutch nationality or something or somebody else. But here the Bible makes it clear that God proposes the grace of the Lord Jesus Christ and the power of the Holy Ghost manifests the image of His dear Son and pleases to manifest His grace, His love, His kindness, His mercy, His heavenly, divine disposition.

If this old disposition is to be taken captive by the Holy Ghost, I am to be so changed in my nature by the power of the Holy Ghost that my life and my attitudes and my words and my deportment become a vehicle of divine expression. Amen.

Brother Barbee tells about a lady that talked to him. "I want to know, Brother Barbee, is this nerves or is this carnality?" she said. "We will be driving down the highway and I will tell my husband to slow down, or to watch out for the light, or to be careful for the pedestrians, or to slow up. The next thing you know, if he does not, my hands are in his hair. When we are talking at the table and we are discussing a problem, I may let fly with something or just let go."

Brother Barbee answered, "Sister, that is nervous carnality."

He did a good job of diagnosing the cause of the trouble. There is a nervous carnality. A lot of folks sit on church boards and in church pews and some of them will go to camp meeting, but they are sour and hard to get along with. They have bad attitudes and bad dispositions. They still shout and then they say, "But we have this treasure in earthen vessels. You cannot expect much of us, brother. After all, this is the way our grandparents were and that is the way we have been from childhood."

But there is a cure. There is a divine remedy. If you are a truly sanctified individual and your nerves push into one kind of trouble or another, right away your heart is grieved because here is a manifestation that is unlike the Master, and it is through purely human channels. Immediately you ask forgiveness. You say, "I am sorry. I want you to forgive me. I want nothing in my life to express anything but the glory of the Master and the power of His presence and a manifestation of His love."

Do you know what I am talking about? Is the life of Jesus manifested in your mortal body?

Let us go to Philippians 1:20. Paul says, "According to my earnest expectation and hope, that in nothing I shall be ashamed, but that with all boldness, as always, so now also Christ shall be magnified in my body, whether it be by life, or by death."

Now Christ is to be manifested and Christ is to be magnified. That means that Christ is to be made clear, that the life of Christ is to be brought into focus in my life, and then that life is to be multiplied and magnified until those that come in contact with me, whether they are seeking my life or seeking my death, may see at all times a holy, divine profile of Christ-likeness in me, in my heart, in my word, in my attitude, in my disposition.

Popish Attitude

I am amazed at the dispositions that can be demonstrated in so-called Christian examples. Yet these Christians go right on with never a twinge of conscience nor a move to humble themselves—with no humbleness of soul.

I believe one proof that an individual is the seed of the devil as far as Christian experience is concerned is the fact that he never humbles himself. He never has anything to confess. He never sees where he could go down in the sight of God. He is infallible. He has a popish attitude about him. He has never done wrong. He has never made a mistake. If anybody has to come with a bowed head it is the other person.

Remember one thing—no matter how you behave you are true to your nature. You say, "Well, that was my nerves or something else." That was your true nature manifesting itself. A fountain does not yield both salt water and sweet. You are true to your nature.

"Everyone that is perfect shall be as his Master." Now it says here, "The disciple is not above his Master." What does that mean? That simply means that you and I are not any better than our Master. But here is the thing that puzzles me. Why is it that most of us expect to be treated better than the Master? Why, we can hardly take anything in the way of criticism or ostracism or misrepresentation or misunderstanding. Right away we are whimpering and sorrowing around and publishing our sad story, putting out a booklet or publishing a paper or advertising to the world. "Look how I am being mistreated. Look what a hard time I am having. Or you do not know how they treated me?"

Did you ever consider how they treated the Master? The disciple is not going to be treated any better than his Master. And as I told you in the beginning, the Master's troubles did not come from the outside but the Master's greatest troubles and heartaches came from the inside.

The Example of the Master

Did you ever stop to consider what they did to Jesus? They hated Him. They hounded Him. Of those that should have welcomed Him, those that should have been looking for His coming, who should have welcomed His appearance, it was said, "He came unto His own and His own received Him not." His own brethren, they doubted Him. His own disciples, they eventually forsook Him and fled. One of them denied Him with a curse and with an oath and another sold Him for thirty pieces of silver.

They eventually drove Him to Golgotha's Hill, they nailed His hands to the cruel cross and put the crown of thorns upon His brow. They smote Him on the face. It was not the Romans—it was those of His own household that filled His beard with their dirty phlegm and their rotten spit. It was those of His own household that laid the lash upon His back and were guilty of all the perfidy and all the lies and licentious ways. Those that should have received Him, those that should have loved Him, those that should have fellowshipped Him were the very ones that hounded Him and hated Him. They hated His piety. They hated His popularity. They drove Him from pillar to post until eventually they crucified the Lord of glory.

But when He was reviled, He reviled not again. And when He was stricken and smitten, He threatened not, though He could have called twelve legions of angels and could have taken care of all His enemies in a mighty swoop of a sword of judgment. He did not threaten. He did not say, "Wait until my day comes. Wait until my time arrives. I will handle you. You will be sorry for what you have done." In the midst of it all He cried out, "Father! Father! Forgive them, they know not what they do."

Over here in the shadows perhaps upon horseback was the centurion. He looked on. The clouds were hanging low. Sackcloth of hair covered the sun. The earth was rocking and reeling and trembling. The Son of God, about to expire, made a tremendous cry, "Forgive, forgive, forgive!"

The centurion smote on his breast and said, "Surely this is the Son of God." Something a sermon never did, something a discourse or dissertation or miracle never performed, was accomplished by the gracious words of forgiveness that poured from the lips of the Son of God while the spear was thrust deep into His side. Even while He was being spit upon by His haters and tormenters, words of love and pity flowed from His lips. No wonder the centurion was being converted.

There is a centurion standing by in your life and maybe he is saying, "I would be a believer if it were not for these believers. I would be a Christian if it were not for these Christians."

Why is it that we expect to be treated better than the Master? Jesus is saying here, "I will tell you how my disciples are going to act. I know how they are going to act."

And then He goes on and draws a contrast between the old law and the new. "It hath been said an eye for an eye and a tooth for a tooth." That was the law of reciprocity. "If you punch me in the eye I have a right to punch you." That is what the Law said. "If you knock out my tooth, I have the right to get your tooth if I can."

But Jesus said, "There is going to be a new law in the nature of mankind. The old law of your natures; your depraved dispositions, is going to be gone, and I am going to put a new law down in there. I am going to put something down in there so that when they hate you, you are going to love them. And when they curse you, you are going to talk about them but you are going to talk to my Father in Heaven, not to others.

"And when they smite you on one cheek you are going to turn the other cheek. And when they bid you go a mile, you will go two miles. If they ask you for your coat, you are going to slip off your cloak as well. And you are going to heap coals of fire upon their heads. You will not repay vengeance for vengeance, because 'vengeance is mine and I will repay,' saith the Lord.

"If your enemy hungers you are going to feed him, and if he is thirsty you are going to give him something to drink. You are not going to be overcome of evil, but you are going to overcome evil with good—the holy, good treasure laid up in your heart by the Holy Ghost."

11
What Follows the Spear?

WHEN THE SPEAR IS thrust at you, what follows the spear? When the spear was thrust into the heart of the Master, out came blood and water, symbolic of an outpoured life and a broken heart. But when the spear is thrust into the side of the average holiness professor today, gall and bitterness and rancor follow the spear.

Oh, yes, we will be punctured all right. We will be stuck, all right. We will be thrust through, all right. But the important thing is, what follows the spear?

The disciple is not above his Master, but the disciple shall be like his Master. The world is full of fighters and smiters, and you are going to be smitten. You are going to meet the pugilistic type. Every church has a few pugilists. Every congregation has a few fighters and smiters, and you are going to be slapped, you are going to be knocked down, sir. Somebody is going to walk all over you. And of course, unless you have the divine nature, something is going to rise up inside of you and say, "Don't you lie down;" or, "Are you going to be yellow?" or, "You could not be a man and take that kind of treatment, could you?"

And if you have the depraved nature, something is going to rise up and you are going to go to retaliating and fighting for your rights. You are going to do a little teeth rattling yourself. You are going to go after a few eyeballs on your own. You are going to fix a few heads. You are going to pull a little hair and sink a few nails in a little deep somewhere.

I am talking now not in a physical sense, but of the spiritual intent of a barbed tongue and of the sharp-tongued attitude of many professors of religion that have depraved nature when they testify to a divine nature.

David's Example

This is illustrated again and again through the Scriptures. I do not want to be long or tedious, but just want to take a quick trip back through the Old Testament—the life of David, for instance. Do you remember David, who went out and slew Goliath? Do you remember David, who took his harp and sat down and played such wonderful music to soothe the temper and the disposition and nature of distraught old King Saul? How lovely he played! But one day after he had slain his enemies, he came back and heard the maidens singing, "Saul has slain his thousands and David has slain his tens of thousands," and was soon made to realize that Saul was eyeing him from that time on.

Saul said to himself, "That is a coming young man. I had better keep my eye on that fellow. And what is more, he can have the kingdom if they are accrediting him with tens of thousands and me with only thousands. I can see the handwriting on the wall."

So he began to carry a javelin or spear for David—just for David. Then one day when David was through playing and about to leave, Saul said, "This is the time. I have had all of this I can take. This thing is going to get out of hand. I had better act in a hurry."

He thrust the javelin, but God was with David and he slipped out of Saul's presence, just as the spear struck quivering in the wall, and lodged in it right where David had been.

You know the story of how Saul eventually went out to hunt for David, on two occasions looking for him on the mountainside. Twice David could have slain Saul. The last time was when Saul was fast asleep with his bolster and bag and cruse of water by his side. David had been hiding in the cave, when lo and behold, he saw his enemy fast asleep.

David's trusty friend, Abishai, was along. He saw Saul fast asleep. "Well, praise the Lord! Hallelujah, David!" he whispered, "Here he is! The Lord has delivered him right into our hands. God has answered prayer. Is that not wonderful? He is right here. Oh, David, let's smite him right now and get it over with."

"Oh, no," David remonstrated, "Touch not the Lord's anointed. Touch not the prophet of the Lord."

"Why, David, you big fool!" Abishai exclaimed. "You are going to let this fellow get away? He is after your life. He would have killed you if he could. He would have finished you. He has tried it again and again. He is pursing you. Now David, surely you canoot see the hand of God in this? David, take a look at my spear. It is sharp, and pointed. I will not really hurt him. Oh, David, let me sink it in deep. Let me stick him good. Oh, David, let me go."

There are a lot of fellows around the country who, if they were in David's shoes, would have said, "All right, boy, but just do not tell anybody that I gave the orders. All right. Let him have it. Bury it in deep, but just keep my name out of this."

No, David said, "Touch not the Lord's anointed. Put up your spear. They that wield the spear will perish by the spear. It may be that he will die at the hands of his enemies, and God will take care of him. If God wants me to be king, he will get me there eventually. I do not want the thing unless God wants me to have it. I am not going to work for it or work my way in or kill anybody to get it. I want God to have His way."

Here was a man that had been hated and hounded and persecuted. He had a chance to retaliate, but he did not. He had a chance to shed blood and do it through the hands of a mediator, but he would not do it. He preserved his enemy. He left his life untaken. He went off and said, "O Saul! O Saul, Saul!"

At this Saul woke out of his sleep. "That sounds like the voice of David—my son David," he said.

Then David called back, "Where is the king's bolster and where is the king's water?"

Saul looked around and at last realizing David had spared his life, he cried, "Oh, David, my son, my son. I know that thou shalt be king in Israel, whereas this day thou hast rewarded me good for evil."

Your Turn

That is it. When you have a chance to thrust it in real deep on somebody else's influence or good name or reputation, what do you do? Especially when he has said things about you. Especially if you know that he has spread some scandal and has slandered your name and maybe has called you a compromiser or a lot of other things that might not be too complimentary. Now it is your turn. Now the wheel has turned. Now it is your chance.

Well, if you have a divine nature you will do just exactly what this thirty-fifth verse tells us God does. He is kind to the unthankful. He lets the rain fall on the just and on the unjust.

12

Joseph and His Brethren

THERE IS ANOTHER CHARACTER in the Old Testament we could mention. A fellow by the name of Joseph. Remember Joseph? How Joseph loved God, and how his father loved him! Joseph had a coat of many colors. His brothers were jealous of him. He came out to get their testimony and to bring a little cheese and to find out how things were going with them, and they said, "Here comes that dreamer—that fellow that says we are going to bow and scrape and all that sort of stuff. What do you say we take care of him this morning?"

A conspiracy was made. He was sold into Egypt as a slave. The beautiful coat of many colors was soaked in the blood of a goat and taken back to the father who immediately cried, "A wild beast has torn him."

Twenty years later there was a famine in the land where Jacob and the brothers lived. They were lean and lank and in pretty bad shape. At last Jacob said, "I hear there is corn in Egypt." You remember that it was in Egypt that Joseph was living.

My brother, it is no strange thing that some people who keep sweet are always fat in their souls. Some folks wonder, "They always seem to find the best clover patch and they always seem to have the biggest corn crop and they always seem to have this and that."

There was corn in Egypt, and Joseph had the corn of Egypt all stacked away. He was well fed and well taken care of.

So the brothers went down, and when they arrived they had their money in hand. They came in before Joseph, and when Joseph saw them he recognized them right away. If he had been like some people he would have said, "I know you birds. You good-for-nothing dirty rats. Kneel! Kneel! You know who I am? I am Joseph! I am the ruler of this whole outfit down here. Now you scum, you crawl. You want grain do you? Pick it up off the floor with your teeth. Come on now. Get down there Judah. Get down there Simeon. Get down there Reuben. Bow or I will call my task masters in to lay the lash on your backs.

"You old good-for-nothing bunch of renegades. You are the fellows that caused me to spend years in jail. I have had an awful time down here, but God has taken care of me. And you scum, now *you* are going to crawl. Remember the stories I told you of the sheaves bowing down and the stars in heaven? Remember that? Now this scripture is fulfilled in your ears this day."

Well, Joseph made himself a little bit strange because he was experiencing mixed feelings. He felt an urge to get a hold of old Reuben and Simeon and to hug them around the neck. But he held himself aloof. It was love planning and love scheming. Before his brother left, he gave instructions to his servants. "Now load these fellows down with all the corn they can carry," he ordered, "all the grain they can carry. And put every man's money in the sack."

I would not be surprised if Joseph did not fill up some of those bags himself. I can almost see him taking a great big scoop shovel, getting down there and filling up this bag full of grain. There he goes. He pours in the grain, and when it gets up near the top Joseph picks up the bag and begins to shake and jounce it up and down. He gets another full shovel scoop, pours a little bit more and then the tears run down his cheeks because he had given a scriptural measure, "pressed down, shaken together," and it is running over. On top of the grain he puts his brothers' money in the sacks and sends them home. Their old camels, their knees buckling, are just swaying on the desert trail, having an awful time trying to make it back to the land of Canaan.

Love's Scheme

For fear he would never see them again Joseph's love came up with a scheme that kept Simeon with him as a prisoner. He said, "I understand you fellows have another brother and you talk about a father and say that you are not spies. Just to prove that you are not spies, I am going to have this fellow stay with me here and the rest of you fellows can go on. If you come back again bring that other brother with you to prove these things to me."

Then Joseph took Simeon, bound him and took him home. I think he made him a prisoner about the house, had him wash a few dishes and sweep a little dirt. At the close of the day down in his office Joseph called Simeon in, and through an interpreter, for he did not want Simeon to recognize who he was, he found out all he could about the old father. "Tell me about the old man," he said. "Tell me about the other brother you left at home. Tell me about these fellows and of their families."

Joseph spent every evening by the fireside talking to his prisoner, being with him, and getting all the information he could.

In due process of time Joseph's father and brothers ran out of corn again. They came back. This time Joseph had an awful time holding onto his emotions. There they were, all in front of him, and he said to the chef, "Hey, kill the fatted calf and put out a big meal. I am going to have these boys home for dinner today." Praise God forever!

When things were ready, Joseph came in and put his brothers right around the table according to their ages. They marveled and wondered about this man that seemed to know so much about them. Besides, Joseph had given Benjamin five times more than he gave anybody else.

When the brothers got their bags all filled full Joseph could not think of any special reason why he should keep somebody there but he knew in his heart that he could not stand to have these fellows all go off and leave him and to never see them again. So he said, "Fill their bags and put my silver cup in that young fellow's bag. I will have a good excuse for bringing the whole crowd back again."

The silver cup was put in. It was buried deep in the grain bag, and off they went. But they had not left the city limits before Joseph was saying, "I cannot stand it. I cannot take it. Go out and bring that crowd of fellows back here."

It was not long before they were all back, and I tell you, they were disturbed. They were all upset. They wondered what was wrong. They were tremendously concerned. They remembered again how they had treated their brother.

The bags were opened up one after another. At last they came to the younger fellow's bag, and sure enough, there was the cup. Joseph could not hold himself any longer. He said, "All you Egyptians get out of here a minute."

Then he said to the others, "I am Joseph. I am thy brother." The Book says they were troubled at his presence. "Our brother!" they exclaimed to one another. "If this is Joseph, what is he going to do to us?"

Class Meeting

The Scripture said he went over and fell on Benjamin's neck. They all began to weep and to cry. Of course Joseph had no trouble loving old Benjamin, for Benjamin had never done him any wrong. Benjamin had always loved him. But what was next? Simeon and Reuben and Judah and the rest of them just did not know what was coming off. But that is not where the verse ends. The Scripture says, "And so did he unto them all."

I would like to have been there when Joseph reached around Judah. I would like to have been there when he put his arms around old Reuben and around old Simeon, the boys who helped plan the conspiracy. I would like to have been on hand, brother. The scripture says, "He wept on their shoulder."

They were troubled at his presence. He said, "Do not chide yourself. You thought it for evil, but God meant it for good. You did not send me down here. God sent me here. God sent me ahead to preserve your lives. God sent me down here to preserve your father and to preserve your sister and to preserve you brothers. God sent me out here."

After they finished embracing, hugging and loving one another, I can see them pushing one another off and looking full into each others' eyes. At last the emotional season was over. The Egyptians had heard the racket. They knew some kind of a closed class meeting was going on, that something was being settled that had hung in the air a long time. You could not keep a thing like that under cover.

Joseph said, "I have a little speech to make. Not only did God send me down here, but boys, there are still five years of this thing left. You do not have enough money up there to pay your way through." And I like this expression. "I have a place over here in the land of Goshen where you can be near to me."

If he had been like a lot of folks I know, he would have said, "Well, I will do you a good turn, but I want you way out here in left field somewhere. I am going to put you out in the back part. I am going to put you out here on hard scrabble." But no, he put them in the land of Goshen where the grass was the highest and the foliage was the greenest and the water was the most abundant, where they were near to him.

Where did you put them, brother? Where did you put them, sister?

It was such a tremendous thing for the brothers that they never did fully accept it. Even after the old father came down and stayed they could never fully grasp it. And when old Jacob died they sent a special messenger over to Joseph and said, "Now, our father said you should treat us very kindly after his death."

The scripture once again says, "Joseph wept," as though he had not said enough; as though he had not done enough; as though he had not manifested enough love. These fellows were pretty hard to convince. He broke down and wept and made the same speech all over again. Hallelujah!

This thing not only forgives, but it keeps forgiving. This thing not only forgives, but it forgets by the help and grace of God, when some other folks want to keep right on remembering. Amen. Hallelujah.

These boys thought that Joseph's soul was as small as theirs, and they said, "When the old man is gone he will revert to his old ways. He will go back. He will be just like we would be if we were in his place."

But Joseph is a type of Christ. He is the type of a Spirit-filled individual. And that is the way, by the grace and help of God, every sanctified soul behaves.

Yes, I would like to have been back in the little tent when those boys came piling in and when all those wagons came rolling up to bring all the utensils and things. I would like to have been there when the boys filed into the old man's tent. They came in and all stood around and Jacob could tell that something was on their minds.

"Well boys, what is on your mind? I see that you are all here. Did you get the grain?"

"Yes, we did."

I can just see them sort of shift back and forth, study the hole in the top of the tent, look at the light streaming in through the side.

"Dad, there is something we would like to tell you. It is going to be rather hard, Dad."

"What is it, boys?"

"Oh, Dad, you know about Joseph."

"Oh, yes. Do not mention Joseph."

"Dad, Joseph is alive."

"Oh, boys, do not play any tricks. You know the mention of his name just hurts me. Do not mention Joseph."

"Joseph is alive."

"He could not be. Right over here, I have kept it for these twenty-two years, there is the old coat you fellows used to be jealous of, you used to be so disturbed about, used to be so upset about. I probably was wrong. I probably did make some mistakes. I am sorry, boys. Do not bring Joseph up."

"Dad, Joseph is alive."

And then they begin to unravel the story how they hated him, how they despised him, and how they sold him. How they did not trust him. How God had elevated him. How glad and magnanimous he was and how he would not take any money from them. How he gave them everything. How he filled the bags full. When they would have starved he fed them. When they were thirsty he gave them drink. When they would have perished he gave them a place to stay. He protected them. He loved them. And what is more, he proved that he forgave them.

No Stones of Retaliation

I just want to mention this one more illustration. I see a picture in the New Testament that I can never forget. I see a young fellow, Stephen by name, preaching a powerful message under the anointing of the Spirit. I see a rabble crowd raised to fever pitch because an intellectual young fellow in the crowd is egging them on—egging them on! At last the crowd begins to gnash with their teeth and to cry for blood. This young fellow is right in the middle of it all urging them on. Saul of Tarsus is his name. He is there. He is offering to hold the garments, to hold the tunics of those that will swing the rocks and throw the dirt.

Now remember, it is Saul of Tarsus that is telling Luke, the beloved physician, years later about this fellow. I can see him as he says, "I stood there holding their garments, each one passing them on to me. I can see Stephen now. As he preaches I see the fire in his eyes. I see the indomitable spirit on his face. Then I give the word, and they begin to throw the stones thick and fast and heavy and hard. One strikes him on the shoulder and another hits him in the side and another lands on his feet and another hits him on the head. Blood begins to spurt, and soon he staggers and falls in a heap.

"Then he gets himself to his knees. And Luke, Luke, I see his face. His face shines like the face of an angel. I hear him say, 'I see Jesus.' I do not see Him. Stephen also says, 'I see the glory.' He is looking steadfastly into heaven when the last rock comes that puts him out of commission, puts him out of business, puts him out of this world."

An arrow landed in that intellect's heart that day, something that all of his intellectual knowledge and ability could never pull out. Something landed. Something really stuck. He could shake the sermon. He could shake the logic of the message. He could shake the theory. But he could not shake that shining face. He met a man with a glory face. He met a man with a glory countenance. He heard him say, "Lord, lay not this sin to their charge."

So much like the words of the Master! So much like the words of Jesus! "I saw his face—the face of an angel."

My dear friends, Stephen looked to heaven when the rocks came. Stephen looked to heaven until he saw Jesus. Stephen steadfastly looked to heaven until his countenance was covered with heavenly radiance and celestial glory. He did not look for a rock to throw back. He did not look for a stone to retaliate. He looked to Jesus.

My dear friends, the times I am most ashamed of in my life are the times when I have failed to manifest the disposition of the Master. Under the sandpaper, when the rub comes, when misunderstanding comes and misrepresentation, when lies by false brethren come, when evil reports come, I am concerned about only one thing—living like the Master. Nothing should grieve us more than to come short of living like the Master.

When I look up and see the tall, straight stature of Jesus, when I see that profile of loveliness, I see what a runt I am, what a pigmy I am. Something in my heart cries out, "Oh, to be like Him. Oh, to be like Him."

PART IV
THE TEN VIRGINS

13

More Alike than Unlike

THIS IS A VERY familiar parable. It is a parable of an oriental wedding. And it is a parable that teaches us individual and personal responsibility at the time of the coming of our Lord.

I am sure I do not need to emphasize the fact that we are living in the end time, that the signs of His return are replete and are on every hand, and that while we may look around and wonder about others— about churches, about schools, about institutions, about denominations, about world movements (whether it is the ecumenical movement headed by the Pope or Eugene Carson Blake or somebody else)— there are all kinds of signs that point to the fact that we are living in the end time. We are in the last days. We are not living in the Saturday night of time. We are living with just a few moments left until the striking of the momentous hour when I believe Jesus Christ will return in power and great glory.

The emphasis of this parable is that you and I, as individuals, be ready—that I be ready, that you be ready. After all, we are not going to be ready as denominations. This is a parable of the kingdom. It is not a parable of your church or my church.

Half of the folks in this parable went through on silvered wings. The other half went to buy something they could not get.

If this is a parable of individual and personal responsibility and five were taken and five were left, while these percentages are not hard and fast, all you have to do is take a good, sharp look across the denominational line or the local line or the family line or the camp meeting line to be made aware that the average professor of religion is not ready for the coming of the Lord.

Now, there are three things I want to mention concerning this parable.

First, I want to talk about the mathematical element. It is found in this parable, for there are five wise and five foolish virgins. It is a parable of ten virgins. It is a parable of ten virgins in relation to the Kingdom of God. It is interesting to notice that the difference between the five wise and the five foolish is not apparent until the very end of the parable. You cannot distinguish the one from the other until you come down to the very end of the parable. They are all virgins. This word *virgin* simply means that they were pure, that they were chaste, they were clean, that they were separated. It means that they were not contaminated. It simply means that here is a replica of the Kingdom of God, and these individuals are genuinely born again. They are virgins. They are in the Kingdom of God.

This is a picture of an Oriental wedding. Here is a picture of a bride and her attendants—those that went in to be with the bride. It is a picture of those that seemed to be ready, and those that were ready; those that were left out and those that went in. It is a solemn and serious thought that some of us could well be left out.

Now, I want you to notice that these five wise and five foolish virgins shared many things in common. As I implied a few moments ago, they were more similar in their relationship than they were dissimilar. They were more alike in all aspects as far as the eye could see than they were not alike.

For instance, they were all virgins. They all had lamps. They all had wicks. They all had fire. They all had on the proper garments. They all slumbered and they all slept. They were very, very similar. They shared a common religious experience, if you please. I have implied that they were all virgins, that they were all in the Kingdom of God, that they all had lamps, that every lamp had a wick, and every wick had some fire. So they all had a common experience.

The Glory of Salvation

Now you do not need to be sanctified holy and baptized with the Holy Ghost to have an experience with a good measure of fire. Really get saved and you have some fire. Really get born again, and you have some fire.

I am afraid sometimes we holiness preachers have emphasized the baptism of the Holy Ghost fire and have so magnified the second experience that we have not given the first work its just and true desert. But it really is a wonderful thing to be born again. It really is a glorious thing to be converted. It really is a tremendous thing to be transported out of the darkness into light. It is a wonderful thing to be brought from spiritual death into spiritual life. That is a great thing. That is no mean thing, brother, when God unearths you and uncovers your sin and your iniquity and brings you into the glorious life of the Son and the radiant sunlight of God.

To me, that was a wonderful experience. Amen. When my name was written down in the Lamb's Book of Life and I could look up and

...*Read my title clear to mansions in the sky,*
I could bid farewell to every fear
And wipe my weeping eyes.
Though earth against my soul engage,
And fiery darts be hurled,
I could smile at Satan's rage
And face a frowning world.

Hallelujah for the new-birth experience! The old Methodist writer put it this way:

I then rose to the sky,
really justified I,
 nor did envy Elijah his seat.
My glad soul mounted higher,
In a chariot of fire,
 And the moon, it was under my feet.

That is a clear experience. That is wonderful.

These virgins shared a common experience, and if you really get converted the Holy Ghost will kindle the fire of divine love on the main altar of your heart. You will have some fire in your prayers and some fire in your testimony and some fire in your preaching and some fire in your services. There will be the characteristic of holy fire.

Lamps and Wicks

We are living in a day when the basic religion is a religion of lamps and wicks. We have a lot of lamps. We have a lot of very fancy lamps hanging around. Oh, they are rather beautiful affairs. We dust them and we brag on them. They are very lovely lamps. Some of them are antiques, and the older they get the more beloved and the more revered they become to us because, after all, we have had them for such a long time and they mean so very much to us.

But I am not talking about lamps. I am talking about the fire. We have lots of fancy lamps, lots of fancy professions, lots of long wicks, but where is the fire? When and if you are genuinely born of the Spirit of God, there is some fire. Glory be to God. There is some fire in the experience.

The average holiness church you go to at the present time is more or less a religion of lamps and a religion of wicks. That is all they have. Everything is so very cold. Everything is so very icy. Everything is so very starchy. The preacher is a well-educated fellow. He has a well-modulated voice that he regulates well. He has a very suave personality. He has a very bland disposition.

Everybody in the church is that way. They are all bland. They are all very calm. They are all very collected. They all walk around in decency and in order. Nobody gets out of the way. The aisles are never jammed with people shouting or their services interrupted by a happy "Hallelujah," or a "Glory be to God." The program is never upset. The timetable is never upset as much as thirty seconds.

Everybody shuffles along right in gait. They wheel and they turn and they salute and they get down and they are at ease. The whole business is done with military regularity. The service is as cold as a top sergeant's voice, just as icy as the top sergeant's stare.

The people are just as straight as cornshocks in the fall, and they are just as dead. It is a well-ordered affair. Everything is in its proper place. It is the religion of lamps and wicks.

When you come in the door they hand you a menu with everything printed in a very fine and legible manner. They have a little bit here, and they have a little nibble there, and in between, of course, they have a little celery to put a little color in the thing. Then they have some warbling affair that does a few flipflops on the high bar of the musical scale, or the choir swings in and out in time to some of the more respectable hymns of the church—the kinds of things we all like to hear. But it is all characterized with a lot of polish.

You can see that they are adjusted to this. There is no sign of dust on this lamp. They have kept this thing in good shape. They polish it assiduously. They really know how to go through all this without a hitch. It is just like fellows out on the parade ground. They know just how to step it off. They know the *Hup, two, three, four. Hup, two, three, four.* They can go through it with their eyes shut. Everything is right there. If there is any noise at all it is just a blank that goes off accidentally, and nobody can get hurt because the preacher's gun is not loaded anyhow.

The Work of Jack Frost

It is just a religion of lamps and wicks. Old Jack Frost has been around to the members of this church doing a nifty little work. He has painted the window panes, he has fixed up everything very attractively, very lovely, very beautifully, and the ice is everywhere. It is thick enough in the aisles that you could skate up and down them. There is a snowman in the pulpit and there are snowballs in the pew. Everything is very rigid. Everything is very frigid. Everything is very icy and nicey.

Everything is according to decency and order. The preacher eventually gets to his *firstly*'s and *secondly*'s and *thirdly*'s and *fourthly*'s, then he has them all stand like orderly little soldiers and he gives them the sweet little benediction. He is at the door to wring their hands, to give them a very gracious smile, to invite them back to the same place next Sunday and to assure them that the temperature will not change, that nothing will disturb them or knock the frost off of them. He assures them there will be no unconscious heat turned on them. He assures them that the thermostat will stay at this low, low key.

But listen, my dear friend, if we have the New Testament experience in our hearts, in the church or wherever we happen to be, there is fire also. Lord, have mercy on us. A religion of lamps and wicks!

14

A Shared Expectancy

THESE FIVE WISE AND five foolish virgins all shared a common experience. They all had the fire. Blessed be God forever. Not only that, but they all shared in a common expectancy. They were all looking for the Bridegroom to come. And naturally with that expectancy they all shared a common excitement. When you have the expectation of taking part in a wedding you also have the excitement that goes along with that expectancy. If you have a part in a wedding it is only natural that you are going to get just a little bit excited as you expect the coming of the bridegroom, even though you are not the bride.

Now, we do not have any girls, but my wife, even though she does not have a daughter to get married someday, can get excited over somebody else's daughter getting married. If, as we are driving down the street in the month of June when weddings happen to be in season, she sees a church door open and somebody in a little frilly thing and what not, she will say, "Oh, Honey, pull over. Let's see if we can see the bride."

We do not even need to know who it is. We may be 700 miles away from home, but she still wants to see if we can see the bride.

Yes, a natural excitement goes with a wedding as far as the one is concerned who has a part in the ceremony. The only girl that really cannot get thrilled is the girl that missed the man the other girl got. No, she cannot really be interested in that kind of an affair. She cannot be thrilled by that kind of an arrangement.

But here are these girls. Here are these members of this bridal party. They share in a common expectancy. They are looking for someone to come.

I am here to tell you, brother, if we share in the common expectancy and excitement that goes with the coming of the Son of God, there will be a tremendous transformation of our attitude. Now, this is the thing that bothers me in my own living, and it bothers me in my own preaching. Though I preach about it, though I pray about it, though I study about it, I sometimes wonder how keenly I really believe in the soon coming of Jesus Christ. Because if I really believed it as deeply and keenly as I ought to, and I think if you believed it as deeply and keenly and intensely as you say you do, I wonder if it would not change our attitudes toward a lot of things that we more or less place a lot of reliance and trust in as far as this present world is concerned.

Real Belief Changes our Attitude

If we really believed that Jesus was coming, I believe that a lot of materialistic things would lose their hold and their grip. They would, no doubt, lose their appeal. A lot of money that is going to certain earthly material things would find its way into the channels of the work of God.

A lot of people are acting as though this world is the center of things, as though this world is the end of things, as though this world is the beginning of things. But, brother, if you believe that Christ is going to come and take His waiting bride away, then you do not believe that this world is the center of things and the beginning of things and the end of things. And if you really do not believe that, then you begin to work and to labor to lay up treasures on the other side where "moth and rust doth not corrupt nor thieves break through and steal." Amen.

If the holiness movement in general believed that Jesus Christ was going to come, if we sincerely believed it way down deep in our hearts, I do not believe we would have any trouble getting folks to get rid of televisions, wedding rings, bobbed hair and abbreviated attire. I do not think we would have much trouble getting that done if they really believed Jesus Christ was going to come. But a lot of folks do not really believe Jesus is going to come—not soon, at least. So they go on living as though they will have plenty of time to repent, plenty of time to get things taken care of. "We are going to eat and drink and be merry and enjoy ourselves today," they say, "and somehow or another we will make it through at the last."

But that is not the attitude of an individual who really believes that Jesus Christ is coming and that His coming is right at the door. Amen.

If we really believed Jesus was coming and that the heathen are going to be lost forever if they are not evangelized, I think we would sell a lot of junk we have. I think we would sell all of our televisions, buy a great big boat, fill that boat with Bibles, populate it with young men and young women, and send that boat around the world, dropping our young people off in the east and the west and the north and the south to evangelize. I think we would do this if we really believed Jesus Christ was coming in the near future. But we do not really believe it.

The virgins shared in the common expectancy. I believe an atmosphere of holy anticipation and excitement goes with the thought that Jesus Christ may come before the dawn of another day. Amen. But, you know, we cannot get excited over the coming of Jesus anymore.

Anticipation of His Appearing

I can remember when a preacher would preach on the second coming of Christ, the crowd would go into pandemonium. I can remember when a fellow would preach on Jesus Christ coming in the clouds with power and great glory; how Jesus Himself will give a mighty shout; how the angel will blow the trumpet; how the trumpet of the Lord will sound and the dead in Christ will rise first; how we which are alive and remain will be caught up with the Lord in the air; how the dormitories of the dead will be shaken; how Abraham and Isaac and Jacob come out of their cave and wipe the sand of the centuries out of their eyes—come out rejoicing, come out shouting. Why, brother, the congregation would be out of their seats. They would be leaping and shouting and praising God in anticipation of a reunion with Abraham and Isaac and Jacob and all the other worthies.

But today we sit like a bump on the bench when it comes to the matter of thinking of Jesus' returning. We more or less say, "Well, now, Lord. You do not need to be in any great big hurry. After all, Lord, it is rather comfortable here. We are enjoying our ranch home, and we have only a couple of more payments on our old bucket of bolts. We are feeling pretty good, and we can put up with arthritis a little while longer. Really, Lord, do not upset your own plans by coming just now. Just do as you please. Of course, we want you to come, Lord. Now do not get us wrong, Jesus. We do love your appearing, and we will be happy when you come. But do not hurry anything up on our account."

Brother, if you and I were to test our readiness for the rapture by the anticipation, by the expectation, by the excitement generated in our hearts, during the ministry of the Word concerning the Second Coming of Jesus Christ, a good many of us would be more or less satisfied not to have our real emotions known. Amen.

Is this not the sad and tragic truth? Is this not a sad commentary on our own state of being spiritually unprepared?

I have heard Brother French preach on this theme a good many times in the past, have heard the crowds shout and have seen folks turn handsprings and climb up the side of the wall and swing around the poles, but I have also heard him preach in other camp meetings, when folk just sit on their hands, because somehow or another there is an unreadiness. They are not thrilled by it.

The Church Grows During Hard Times

It was interesting looking at some statistics the other day which were released by the editor of a certain church paper. He made it very clear that the time and the period of the greatest growth in his church was during World War II—is that right? No, that is false. Well, the time of the greatest growth in that church was during the Korean War? No, wrong again. The time of the greatest growth was during the advent of radio? No, wrong again. When was the time of their greatest growth as a church? When did they have more preachers, percentage wise, and more churches, percentage wise? When was it? When the depression was at its highest, and when the economic situation in America was at its lowest.

That was the time when the church experienced its greatest revivals and its greatest increase. And that was true of all the churches in the holiness movement. That was pretty much true clear across the country.

That was when preachers would preach on the Second Coming

and folks would be blessed. They did not have a beefsteak to go home to or a couple of deep freezes to ponder over as to which lid they would raise first. They did not have to wonder whether they would have chicken or whether they would have duck, whether they would have gosling or goosling, whether they would have fowl or whether they would have fish or whether they should have beans, whether they should have strawberries or raspberries or whether it should be blackberries. What a difficult and complex age we have got ourselves into.

But, brother, in depression days—I remember, I was not saved then; I was still in my bootlegger father's home—I can remember they went back home from church to beans and prunes, and prunes and beans. During that time the churches were enjoying revival. Folk came to meeting and sat on hard benches, if they sat on benches at all (they worshipped in little places here and there), and when the "Amen" was given, they would go home to an isolated bean swimming around in a half gallon of water.

When the preachers would preach on the glories of the Second Coming and a deliverance from this world and its corruption and its sin and its sickness and its heartache and its poverty, brother, no wonder they felt like swinging from the rafters and doing circles around the trees and chasing one another around the building. They were not so fat and overstuffed in those days but what they could do it with considerable alacrity. But today, we are so fat. We are feeding and faring sumptuously every day. We are so satiated with materialism and so satisfied with our earthly goods, we are so contented with what we have that there is no romance in leaving this world. It is more or less of a hardship to think of saying good-bye to all of our comforts, conveniences and other earthly and materialistic things we have surrounded ourselves with: "Well, Lord, we can go, but it will almost be a sacrifice to go to heaven."

I do not think we are going to make it if that is the way we are feeling about it. Now, maybe I am wrong. Maybe I have overdrawn the picture, but I think not.

I can remember when I got in this salvation my soul was thrilled at the thought of Jesus' Second Coming. And something is wrong with you and me if we do not get thrilled every once in awhile just in anticipation, in expectation. Amen.

Brother, let me tell you. You take a young fellow that is in love with a young lady, and they are engaged to be married—why, he does not have to have somebody poke him in the ribs and say, "Hey, hey, look, look. Look, she has come in."

Why, even if he happens to be at the far end of the house, he can almost sense her presence when she walks in the door. Something happens to that fellow. Why, when she walks in he is suddenly a different kind of a lad. What has happened? Someone has come. A presence has walked in. He walks around just tingling all over. He is full of excitement. His eyes begin to sparkle. He is just a different fellow. He could have been listless and lop-eared and lolly-goggled and sort of hanging around with no interest in anybody or anything. But let her step in, and all of a sudden he begins to adjust his tie and to shine his shoes on the back of his pant leg, and to put himself in a knot. If he has a little *cologna de horse* he will spray himself a little and make himself smell rather nice. And he will sashay forth because, after all, he wants to do this thing in proper style. You do not have to crank him up or drop a nickel or a dime or a quarter in, or give him a pep talk of any kind. Brother, this thing just goes on.

Somehow or another a good many people have lost the thrill of expectancy in reference to the coming of Jesus Christ. And I am here to tell you, brother, whether or not your soul gets thrilled in this anticipation is one of the most severe tests a man can place on his own soul. When I study and contemplate the coming of Jesus does my heart swell up within me? Does my soul reach out in eagerness? Do my eyes look forward with longing? Is there a quickening of my spirit as I contemplate the face to face confrontation and reunion with my blessed Lord and Savior, Jesus Christ? Does this thing tingle me? Does this thing inspire me? Does this thing thrill me? Does this thing challenge me? Or am I left with somber thoughts and second thoughts such as, "Well, He need not be in a hurry to get here at the present time."

15

The Time of Night

ANOTHER ELEMENT MENTIONED IN this Scripture is a very common one. It is the *time* element: "And at midnight the cry was made."

Now, some very interesting and important events took place at night. For instance, the crossing of the Red Sea took place at night. God sent the pillar of fire to lead the children of Israel across the sea. Yet the Divine Presence was darkness to the Egyptians. It was night to the Egyptians. All night long, while the fiery, cloudy pillar led the children of Israel across the Red Sea, the Egyptians just wandered around in the darkness and waited until morning. It was already morning as far as the children of Israel were concerned, but the crossing of the Red Sea took place at night.

Also, the birth of the Son of God took place at night. It was a clear night. It was a bright night. It was a shining night, and the stars were out. Yes, more than that, the angel choir came and sang, "Glory to God in the highest and on earth peace, good will toward men." It was a glorious and wonderful night when Jesus Christ came into this world.

Other important events took place at night. The Scripture says, "And at midnight a cry was made. Behold the bridegroom cometh."

I am not contending that this was a physical night. I believe this is the symbolism, and I believe it is going to be nighttime when Jesus Christ comes, not a physical nighttime, but it will be a nighttime politically. It will be a nighttime morally, and it will be nighttime spiritually when Jesus Christ comes.

Now, friend, all I ask is, "Are we experiencing a political night?" It seems as though a blackout has more or less struck the minds of the leaders of the world. They are all in confusion. Pick up the newspaper and notice what kind of a dilemma we are in, whether it is in Laos or in Vietnam or the Congo. We have made it ourselves. We have made our own horrible mistakes from one end of this bloody earth to the other.

We have stumbled and fallen. It is nothing but a political night. And there is nobody on the horizon to show us the way out. There is no leader on the scene that can show us what to do. The political magicians are working on the "one church" idea that is supposed to put everybody under one roof. We are going to have one Bible. We are going to have one church one of these days, you know. It is not so far off. We are all going to fall in line. All the apostate Protestants are going to do it.

Yes, it is all part of a political potpourri that is planned for us. But before the political night is crystallized something is going to happen. Jesus Christ is going to make Himself known. Hallelujah! He is going to let them go on stirring their pot and working up their cauldron and mixing their bitter brew, but one day He is going to come back and straighten the while thing out, and He is not going to come back alone. He is going to come back with the blessed and dear children of God.

First, however, this thing is going to get darker and darker. You do not need to look for a Republican to pull us out. I do nor think you can expect any Democrat to pull us out. There is not a politician that knows his way out of the wilderness world that we are in. We are getting in deeper and deeper and deeper, and, brother, I would not be surprised to pick up the morning paper and read, "World War III has started.. The holocaust is on its way and the fires are burning." We are living in a time of unprecedented political darkness and blackness that has covered the eyes of the leaders until here we are. Here we are in America, the land of the free and the home of the brave. Here are our political leaders all blind to the sellout, so blind to Communism they are walking right in. They are handing America and its freedom and its potential and its power right over into the Communists' hands on the right hand and on the left side. Nothing but blind stupidity. Yes, it is a political night.

Moral Nighttime

But it is also a moral night we are facing. Brother, the moral darkness has settled over not only America but the world. Think of the tremendous moral darkness that covers this sad and tragic land of ours! How dark, how low the moral standards are. Somebody some time back conducted a survey and found that over 90% of the boys in a certain senior class and 75% of the girls in that class were drinking alcoholic beverages.

I picked up a paper which told of a 17-year-old girl who died of arsenic poisoning. She and other teenagers had gone out to a party. In the process of their evening, they had a lovely time and drank a little wine. But this wine had been spiked with arsenic. The girl died the next day.

It is a customary thing for young people to drink. It is customary for them to have their PJ parties. It is customary at colleges for the students to mix all of the keys to the girls' dormitory rooms, put them in an open hat, and then for each boy to take out a key. He spends the night with the girl whose door his key fits. We are living in a moral cesspool of iniquity.

If you think I am lying to you, ask anybody who lives around a college. Ask anybody who lives in a college town. How rotten! How full of flowing sewage and impurities and filth the moral system of America is. If you think I am exaggerating that, go and talk to the principal of a public school. Go and talk to some of the superintendents in some of the schools around the country. And you will get one of the saddest and most sordid stories of sadism and immorality and vice ever told. God have mercy upon us.

The moral picture in this country is so dark that, as I read the other day, we have ministers, we have doctors, we have lawyers that have founded what is known as "The Homosexual Society of America."

One day we felt the teaching profession was a high elevated profession, and the teacher stood second only to the preacher for moral veracity and courage in any community. Now it is a common thing for the man teachers in the public school to be immoral with the girls in their classes, to have vice rings, sex rings, crime rings. Almost anything the mind can imagine, you will find some member of the faculty sponsoring in a clandestine manner.

From north to south, from east to west, at one time you could say the rural areas were pretty well sheltered, but today with the advent of the television and the radio and the automobile and all the rest, the sewage from Hollywood and the low morals that we have that started in the gutter, have now inundated not only our school systems but our political system until we have a boggy, soggy, sewer swamp from the White House in the north to the Gulf of Mexico in the south, from the Atlantic on one side to the Pacific on the other. Wherever American servicemen go they carry their venereal diseases, they carry their sin, they carry their iniquity. The entire world, sad to say, at the present time is almost a madhouse of barnyard morals and insane immorality.

When is this Bridegroom going to come? He is going to come at nighttime. And, brother, it is mighty dark out there. If you do not think it is dark all you have to do is to make a mistake at the counter and let the clerk give you back five cents too much or five dollars too many. When you say, "I am sorry, you gave me a nickel too much," she will say, "A nickel too much? Don't you think anything of that. I am surprised. You are the first person to do that. It really is not necessary. It was my mistake."

They think you are crazy if you have any standards of honesty or morality or decency. The average man of the world thinks that after all, swapping wives and living high, wide, and handsome and getting all you can for nothing and cheating the government and beating everybody else is part of living by your wits. That is part of being really sharp at the present time and up to date. That shows you are a real comer. That shows you are a real climber. That shows you are on your way up. But he is mistaken.

Spiritual Nighttime

It is spiritual night. Yes, it will be not only a moral night, not only a political night, but is going to be a spiritual night when the Bridegroom comes.

Notice, the five foolish virgins said, "Our lights are going out." I want to tell you, brother, the lights are going out around the country. The lights are going out around the world.

While you and I are basking in the radiance of God's blessing, call to remembrance the little lighthouse you are attending from Sunday to Sunday. I want to point out the great mistake of professing holiness people who are sitting in little cold churches. Their pastor is a holiness man, who knows the doctrine, who knows everything that goes with it. But, brother, the light is going out. The church used to be filled with fire and holy joy. The altars were lined with sinners finding God. The prayer meetings were red hot times when sinners would get saved and seek the Lord. The meetings were interrupted by happy Hallelujah-Harry's shouting up and down the aisle, or the Glory-to-God-Mary's taking off on a Holy Ghost spell around the meeting house somewhere. But, brother, the lights are going out.

People write me from around the country and say, "Brother Schmul, we are moving to such and such a town. Can you tell us if there is a live church in that town? Can you tell us if there is a spiritual church in that town?"

They do not say, "Is there a Wesleyan Methodist Church in the town, or a Pilgrim Church in the town, or a Nazarene Church in the town, or a Free Methodist Church in the town." They say, "Is there a live church in the town?" Some towns have live Pilgrim churches. Some towns have live Wesleyan churches. Some towns have live Nazarene churches, and so on. But brother, it is getting harder and harder across the years to find a church that has a light, to find a church that has the fire, to find a preacher that carries a burden, to find a pastor that has the fire on his soul. And a lot of people are now wondering, "What should I do? Where should I go? I do not want to leave this high, fashionable steepled place with its fine reputation. After all, I have been in such and such a church all my life. I am a third generation this-or-that. Maybe I am a fourth or fifth-generation member. And, too, what will people say? What will people think?"

I want to know, "What is Jesus Christ to say, and what is He going to think in that day when you and I stand before Him with nothing but a lamp—the fire and the light gone out?"

Flickering Lights in the Darkness

Brother, the lights are going out. We might as well face it. The old-line holiness denominations—their light is flickering in the darkness of the hour when the light is most desperately needed. In some churches the light has almost completely gone out. They have been so worked upon by the forces of darkness and blackness of these last days, they have so compromised, they have so adjusted to the world, that the fire is out and there they stand, a splendid hulk. The outside lovely and glittering, but the inside is burned out. The glory is gone.

As far as I am concerned, brother, you would be better off to go down on the street and worship in it, if you had nobody there but an old snaggled-toothed grandma and a little hunched-back boy, but you had God's presence and you had God's glory—you would be far better off there, I say, than to stay in the high-steepled outfit, let your light go out, be smothered, and lose your family and your soul in the end. Amen.

No use pretending, carrying on as though the church were in good shape. She is not. She is dying. Unless she has a hypodermic shot of a real red-hot revival and has it in a hurry, it is going to take more than your little committee or denominational pull to put her back on her feet again. It is going to take more than a new paint job and a new pair of shoes and a little do-her-up here and a little un-do-her over there. It is going to take a real revolutionary revival that starts at the top and goes to the bottom if the church ever really comes out of it. I am afraid this is the fatal seizure, apart from a Holy Ghost revival. Amen.

Lamps are going out. The school lights are out. Institutions and churches that once were a flame of fire—their lights are going out. They are gutted. They have been gutted by compromise, by lowered standards, by relinquished holy convictions. They have sold out the things they used to contend for, and they have made a trashy deal. They have made a bargain with Assyrians, Egyptians and anybody else, and have borrowed the methods of the Philistines. They have junked the program of God. They are going to move God's cart on their own modernized, mechanized wagon, and they are going to do it in their own way. Amen. Yes, lamps are going out.

16

The Tragedy of the Time

THERE IS AN ELEMENT of *tragedy* in this parable. When the cry, "Go ye forth to meet Him," was made, the lamps were going out. They turned to the five wise and said, "Give us of your oil. Our lamps are going out." At the tragic moment they said, "Give us of your oil."

But the five wise said, "No. You go to those that sell and buy some for yourselves." And while they went to buy the bridegroom came. Eventually, they came back. They knocked on the door. They cried, "Lord, Lord, it is dark. Open to us." And here is the tragedy. From within a voice said, "The door is shut. I know ye not. Depart from me." What a tragic element that is. "The door is shut."

We face a solemn responsibility as individuals. Most of us profess some measure of grace and of God. Most of us profess having some form of godliness and religion. But, my dear friend, how many of us have a sufficiency of the divine supply of Holy Ghost oil to carry us through this tragic period of waiting?

"And they all slumbered and slept." That was the natural process. But the time came when it was necessary to have the goods. And that was to have another cruse of oil with oil in it——another vessel with oil for their lamps.

Instead of paying the price, instead of being fully and totally and completely prepared, these sad, foolish and imprudent individuals did what? They depended on somebody else. The night was longer than they had anticipated, the night was darker than they anticipated, and the bridegroom tarried longer than they had expected. They presumed upon the mercies of God. They presumed upon the circumstances of their day. They just figured they would be able to make it. They just calculated that somehow or another they would come out alright. They knew there was not very much oil left in their lamps, but they thought they would have enough to last—enough to get by.

Let me tell you, my dear friends, you and I had better not go presuming. You and I had better not only have the fire burning on the altars of our hearts, but we had better have a full supply of gospel oil—the Holy Ghost baptism, not only a saving from our sins but a glorious filling of the Holy Ghost.

There are a lot of folks whose supply of spiritual oil is running dangerously low. There are folks who at one time were a fiery flame of holy love and passion and devotion to Jesus Christ but who now carry lamps that are flickering out. Their lights are going out. And when the bridegroom comes they will be snuffed out in a moment. It will be too late. They are going to cry, "Lord, open to us. Open to us." But the door will be closed. The door will be shut.

What a tragic thing, friends. What a tragic thing to come right up to this time and find the door shut when you have spent your time with a group such as the five wise virgins were. Yes, the five foolish worshipped with the five wise. They were in the same fellowship and in the same company. They dressed in the same manner. They enjoyed the same things. They went to the same places. They attended the same camp meetings and the same conventions. They heard the same preachers but, brother, the real distinction was not seen until the very time the door was shut.

Standards will not Save

We have folks that are depending upon a lot of things. Brother, you will have to have more than long sleeves and long hair and the absence of television in your home if you are going to be included in this crowd that is going up. I know folks that have long sleeves that have a long tongue. I know folks that have long hair that have a long reputation for being hard to get along with. I know folks that do not have televisions nor a lot of other things, but they do not have any glory either.

We travel together. We look alike. We talk alike. We shout alike. We sing alike. We are found in the same camp meetings. But one of these days Jesus Christ is going to come and there will be some sad and sorry revelations in that day. Some of you folk are going to come right up to it at the very last and despite what you have not and despite what you have, you are not going to have a sufficiency of divine grace. You are not going to have the fullness of the Holy Ghost. Your spiritual supply will be exhausted. You are going to miss that glorious event—the rapture. God help us here.

I went to the door of a certain party the other day. If I mentioned her name most of you would know her husband at least. He is known all over the country. I knocked on the door. The door opened. The man I wanted to see was not there. And so we engaged in a few moments' conversation with the door open. This woman, whose husband is a very eminent and outstanding preacher and she herself is noted for her eminent and pious life, said to me, "You know, Brother Schmul, I am afraid I am not going to make it. I am afraid I am not going to be ready when Jesus comes."

I said, "My dear sister, I know not only how you feel, but I know that in my heart there is a wonderful, 'Oh God, don't let me get caught in the drift of this day so as to miss it.'"

Brother, I do not know of anybody that can sit down and take it easy and feel as though he has made it. One of the confessions in Robert Murray McCheyne's book is, "One of my temptations is to feel that I am now a mature Christian. And that I am pretty well immune from falling."

Brother, I am here to tell you that none of us are mature Christians, and nobody has it really made and nobody is really settled. I have a fear for you if you do not have a fear for yourself. A good brother said to me recently, "You know, Schmul, you and I could miss it."

I do not have any intentions of missing it, but we can miss it. We can get so busy with everything else that we fail to keep the measure of our spiritual supply full, fail to keep our experience up to the level of a divine runover or splashover.

The disciples were sanctified in the Upper Room on the day of Pentecost, we are told in Acts 2, but in chapter four they are on their knees again, praying the same kind of prayer and the same thing happens. They are all filled with the Holy Ghost. They were not re-sanctified, but they were maintaining the level of their spiritual supply at the full mark.

I am concerned about a good many professors of holiness that let the level of their supply get so dangerously low. They just about stagger into one camp meeting from another and into one convention from another. What if Jesus Christ would come between conventions or between camp meetings or between conference sessions? Sad to say, they would be left on the outside. They would be standing at the door that could never be opened.

Members of Schmul's Wesleyan Book Club buy these outstanding books at 40% off the retail price.

Join Schmul's Wesleyan Book Club by calling toll-free:
800-S$_7$P$_7$B$_2$O$_6$O$_6$K$_5$S$_7$
Put a discount Christian bookstore in your own mailbox.

Visit us on the Internet at
www.wesleyanbooks.com

You may also order direct from the publisher by writing:
Schmul Publishing Company
PO Box 776
Nicholasville, KY 40340

Made in the USA
Columbia, SC
16 March 2018